Sundance, My Uncle

by Donna B. Ernst

THE EARLY WEST
Creative Publishing Company
Box 9292, Ph. 409-775-6047
College Station, Texas 77842

Ernst, Donna B., 1946-
Sundance, My Uncle / by Donna B. Ernst
p. cm. --(The Early West)
     Includes bibliographical references and index.
     Summary: A biography of the notorious outlaw, Harry A. Longabaugh, better known as the Sundance Kid.
ISBN 0-932702-96-1
     1. Sundance Kid--General literature. 2. Outlaws--West (U.S.)--Biography--General literature. 3. West (U.S.)--Biography--General literature. [1. Sundance Kid. 2. Outlaws. 3. West (U.S.)--Biography.] I. Title II. Series

F595.S94E76 1992
364.1'55'092--dc20
[B]
92-34603
CIP
AC

The Mystery Continues . . .

The search for Butch Cassidy and the Sundance Kid began even before Paul Newman and Robert Redford ran into the hail of bullets and glory in the popular movie, Butch Cassidy and the Sundance Kid. While there were many moviegoers who assumed that the end had come for the two outlaw friends, there were already western historians and buffs who claimed Bolivia was not the end for them. Two authors, one of them Butch Cassidy's sister, claim that Butch returned to the United States and lived to be an old man. Author Ed Kirby thinks Sundance returned to the States as well.

When historian Dan Buck worked in Bolivia for the Peace Corps, he became interested in finding out the truth. He and his wife Anne Meadows followed up leads and searched records looking for the two outlaws throughout South America. Their search finally lead them to San Vicente, Bolivia.

Now one of the mysteries about Sundance and Butch may end. Dan Buck has been quoted as saying that although all the witnesses to the 1908 Bolivian gun battle have died, the son of one of the witnesses led them to the house in San Vicente and to graves where the two outlaws were purportedly buried.

Historians Buck and Meadows were part of a successful expedition that resulted in bringing back the remains of the two men from Bolivia to the United States. An announcement is expected sometime during the spring of 1993 concerning the findings of Dr. Clyde Snow, a world-renown forensic pathologist. Dr. Snow was the scientific leader of the expedition to Bolivia, and the two skeletons are now being studied in his Norman, Oklahoma, laboratory.

3

Harvey Sylvester Longabaugh, the fourth child and older brother of Harry, Alias the Sundance Kid. (Courtesy Sundance Properties.)

Table of Contents

*Donna and Paul Ernst, the author and her husband
who is the great-nephew of Harry A. Longabaugh.
(Courtesy Sundance Properties.)*

Author's Preface

Twenty years ago, not much was known about Harry A. Longabaugh, alias the Sundance Kid. Hollywood produced a classic when "Butch Cassidy and the Sundance Kid" hit the screens; but still not much was known about Harry A. Longabaugh. Robert Redford wrote a book, *The Outlaw Trail*, inspired in part by his acting role as the Sundance Kid; and still nothing new had surfaced about who Sundance really was.

Today, however, everyone seems to *know* all there is to find out about Sundance. It's too bad that much of what has been written has been incorrect, with the misinformation of the first author being quoted verbatim by the next, and so forth.

While many family members, including myself, had never heard of Uncle Harry the outlaw, there were a few members of the distant cousins' families who did know much more than we did. After much research and correlating of material from all the "long-lost" relatives, the true story of who Harry A. Longabaugh, alias the Sundance Kid, really was can be written.

I make no apologies or excuses for the kind of life Uncle Harry led; I only want history to include as accurate and as complete a picture as possible. Still today there are family members who do not admit their relationship to Sundance, apparently ashamed of him. But he was a part of history, and he is a part of my family heritage.

There are many people who helped and encouraged me, including relatives, friends, and numerous

7

librarians. Some of them, however, deserve a special mention of thanks. First, to my husband Paul for his constant love, hours of research and red eyes, and continuous discussion and encouragement. Then to my daughters, Jennifer, Susan and Janice, for their patience, support, and proofreading.

A special thanks also goes to my sister, Derri Benbow, for her hours of editing and constructive criticism. I appreciated the hours of research and encouragement given also by Bill and Dot Longabough, Harry and Frances Longenbaugh, Irvin and Lola Longenbaugh, June Head, Kerry Ross Boren, Mary Garmen, Dan Buck, Anne Meadows, many NOLA and WOLA members, Jim and Theresa Earle, Doug Engebretson, and Mr. Thomas Wathen of CPP/Pinkerton, Inc. And thanks to the many who encouraged me just by asking how things were going.

Donna B. Ernst

Part One

Spring, 1867 — Harry A. Longabaugh born in Pennsylvania

August 30, 1882 — left for the West, settled in Colorado

Summer, 1886 — worked for the N - N Ranch in Montana

February 27, 1887 — stole a horse in Sundance, Wyoming

June 7, 1887 — arrested in Miles City, Montana

August 5, 1887 — sentenced 18 months in prison, Wyoming

June 24, 1889 — Telluride Bank robbery, Colorado

*Josiah Longabaugh with his youngest
child, four-year old Harry A. Longabaugh.
(Courtesy Sundance Properties.)*

Chapter One

The Beginning

Family tradition says that two brothers named Lanabach came from Germany and fought with George Washington at Valley Forge in the Revolutionary War. In tracing the family genealogy, a Baltzer and Elizabeth Lanabach began one branch of the family in Hagerstown, Maryland.[1] This branch eventually moved through Illinois and Ohio and then on to Colorado.

Uncle Harry's branch began with a teenaged, indentured servant named Conrad Langebach. He arrived December 24, 1772 in Philadelphia, Pennsylvania, on the Brig *Morning Star* out of Rotterdam.[2] His contract was bought by John Hunter of Chester County, Pennsylvania.[3] The contract called for Conrad to work as an apprentice for five years or to buy his freedom for 28 pounds. Conrad later served at least two months with the militia in Northampton County, Pennsylvania, during the Revolutionary War.[4]

In 1781 Conrad married Catharina, and they settled in New Hanover, Montgomery County, Pennsylvania.[5] They had a large family, and one son was Jonas, born in 1798.[6] Jonas married Christiana Hillbert, and they had six children.[7] One of their children was Josiah, born June 14, 1822, in Montgomery County, Pennsylvania.[8]

Annie Place Longabaugh, the mother of Harry A. Longabaugh. (Courtesy Sundance Properties.)

Josiah married Annie G. Place on August 11, 1855, in Phoenixville, Pennsylvania.[9] She was born September 27, 1828, the daughter of Henry Place and Rachel Tustin of Phoenixville.[10] Josiah and Annie moved frequently, never owned property, and always stayed near Phoenixville where their families lived. Josiah was a common laborer, often hiring out for farm work. He was drafted for the Civil War and was later granted a pension for *General Debility* when he was 69 years old.[11] Josiah and Annie Longabaugh had five children.[12]

Elwood Longabaugh, the brother of Harry A. Longabaugh, in his early twenties. (Courtesy Sundance Properties.)

The first child was Elwood Place Longabaugh, born June 21, 1858, in Mont Clare, Pennsylvania. He died unwed on May 11, 1930, in San Francisco, California, where he had lived for almost fifty years. He was a sailor on whaling ships and worked for a sailor's rooming house.[13] The Pinkerton records indicate that his younger brother Harry visited him occasionally.[14]

Samanna Longabaugh was born April 22, 1860, in Phoenixville, Pennsylvania. She married Oliver Hallman, an ornamental wrought-iron businessman, and they had five children.[15] Samanna died in 1920 at her home in Mont Clare, Pennsylvania. One of her grandsons has her papers and family Bible, but he does

Samanna, standing and Emma, sisters of Harry A. Longabaugh. (Courtesy of Sundance Properties.)

not want to have anything to do with his great-Uncle Harry's infamous reputation.

The next child was Emma T. Longabaugh, born in 1863 in Zieglersville, Pennsylvania. Emma was a seamstress for Wanamakers Department Store and a dressmaker and co-owner of McCandless and Longabough of Philadelphia. She changed the spelling of her name because of her brother's growing reputation. She died unwed January 23, 1933, after disinheriting Sundance in her will.[16]

Harvey Sylvester Longabaugh was born May 19, 1865, in Upper Providence Township, Pennsylvania. He married Katherine Gercke in 1886, and they had three children. Only one of their children lived to adulthood, their son William Henry Longabaugh. Bill married Rose Sophie Sipple, and they had three children, one of whom was Florence Catherine Longabough, the mother of the author's husband Paul Ernst. Therefore, Harry A. Longabaugh, alias the Sundance Kid, was the great-great uncle of Paul Ernst.[17]

The last child born to Josiah and Annie was Harry A. Longabaugh, born in the spring of 1867. At the time of Harry's birth, Pennsylvania did not require birth records, so the exact date and place are unknown. Since the family was Baptist, which does not practice infant baptism, there are no church records either.[18] Verification was made by census records as well as family records and memories.

The 1860 census records show the family, with only Elwood and Samanna, living in a hotel in Trappe, Pennsylvania. This hotel was a stagecoach stop on one of the main roads to Philadelphia and was also run as a boarding house.[19] By the 1870 census, the family was living in Port Providence, a small village in Upper Providence Township, Pennsylvania. Young Harry was named among the children and was listed as being three years old at the time.

The 1880 census listed Harry as being 13 years old. Samanna was married and no longer living with Josiah and Annie. Elwood was listed as being unwell and *living at home;* Emma was also listed as *living at home.* Harvey, aged 15, and Harry were not living with the family in Phoenixville. They were both apparently earning room and board away from the home and family. Harry was found listed as a *hired servant* and *boarding* with Wilmer Ralston and his family in West Vincent,

W. 48693

I, EMMAN T. LONGABAUGH, single woman, being of sound disposing mind, memory and understanding, do hereby make and publish this as and for my last will and testament, hereby revoking and making void all former wills by me at any time heretofore made.

FIRST:- I order and direct my just debts and funeral expenses to be paid as soon as convenient after my decease. The proceeds of the policy of Insurance on my life, now held by Mrs. Samanna Hallman, to be used to pay my said funeral expenses and if such proceeds are insufficient, my Executor, hereinafter named, is to pay the balance thereof.

SECOND:- I give and bequeath all my household goods, furnishings, ornaments, pictures, books, clothing and jewelry to my said sister Mrs. Samanna Hallman, absolutely.

THIRD:- I order and direct my executor hereinafter named to sell all real estate of which I may die seized. The proceeds of which are to be and form part of my residuary estate hereinafter mentioned.

FOURTH:- All the rest, residue and remainder of my estate I give and bequeath as follows:

(1) One-tenth of said residuary estate to the Womens American Baptist Home Mission Society absolutely.

(2) One-half of the remainder of my said residuary estate to my said sister Mrs. Samanna Hallman absolutely

(3) The other one-half of the balance of my said residuary estate to be equally divided between my brothers

Elwood Longabaugh absolutely and Harvey Longabaugh absolutely and in the event of my brother Elwood dying before my death his share is to be equally divided between my said sister Mrs. Samanna Hallman and my said brother Harvey Longabaugh.

(Note: On account of my not knowing whether or not my brother Harry Longabaugh is living, and to avoid any difficulty in settling my estate, I made no bequest to him. This note is merely explanatory, and whether my said brother Harry be living or dead, is not to change or affect this will)

AND LASTLY, I nominate, constitute and appoint CLARENCE L. MITCHELL to be the Executor of this my last will testament.

IN WITNESS WHEREOF I have hereunto set my hand and seal this *Nineteenth* day of *Sept.* *hev* A. D. 1918.

Emma T. Longaba (SEAL)

Signed, sealed, published and
declared by the above named
testatrix as and for her last
will and testament, in the presence
of us, who in her presence, at her
request and in the presence of each
other have hereunto subscribed our
names as witnesses.

Isabel M. Lowry
4870 Hazel Ave. Phila.

Morris M. Paretts
1703 North Eleventh St. Phila.

The Will of Emma T. Longabaugh, sister of Harry A. Longabaugh, alias The Sundance Kid. (Courtesy Sundance Properties.)

Pennsylvania. Mr. Ralston farmed over 100 acres along what is now Route 113, and was about ten miles from where Harry's parents were then living.[20]

Harry's was a relatively poor family. While Harry may have learned to enjoy opera and the arts as an adult, the closest he came to first-class living in his youth was through the books he must have read. He had his own library card, issued on January 31, 1882, for $1.00, by the Young Men's Literary Union in Phoenixville.[21]

On Sundays the entire family attended church together at the First Baptist Church of Phoenixville. The church at Church and Gay Streets was located just across the street from their home in 1882. Annie's parents, Harry and Rachel Place helped establish the church. In fact, Annie's father was a respected deacon of the church, and he would have been very proud that his two granddaughters chose to be baptized as young teenagers.

The extended family in the area included all of Harry's grandparents, many aunts and uncles, and a large number of cousins. It was not at all unusual for them to get together for a picnic or someone's birthday. Harry had a very unsettled spirit, a wanderlust, and he did not feel close to these relatives.

Harry was mothered by his oldest sister Samanna when he was young. They grew extremely close and remained so even after Samanna married in 1878. During school vacations Harry occasionally stayed with Samanna. He enjoyed playing with Samanna's small children and took them for piggyback rides up Hallman Hill or down to the river behind their house. Harry pointed out his Grandfather Longabaugh's house across the river and the top of his Uncle Michael's feed store at Church and Main Streets in Phoenixville. The children adored their Uncle Harry.

Samanna kept some business books for her husband and made occasional notations among the purchase orders. One of her entries reads, *Phoenixville June 1882 - Harry A. Longabaugh left home to seek employment in Ph. and from their (sic) to N.Y.C. from their (sic) to Boston and from their (sic) home on the 26 of July or near that date.* A subsequent notation stated *Phoenixville Aug. 30th 1882 Harry A. Longabaugh left home for the West. Left home at 14 - Church St. Phoenixville below Gay St.* [22] Harry moved west with his cousin George Longenbaugh.

George Longenbaugh was a descendant of Baltzer and Elizabeth. He and his family lived in Shelby County, Illinois. They decided to move West to Colorado in a covered wagon.[23] George invited young Harry to join them, and he accepted. Harry was undoubtedly a big help to George, his pregnant wife Mary, and two-year-old Walter. They arrived in Durango, Colorado and began homesteading. George raised and bred horses, and Harry worked right beside him.

Notes

1. 1776 Maryland State Census Records, Elizabethtown, Frederick County, Maryland, pages 56, 57, 60, and 63; 1790 U.S. Census Records, Washington County, Maryland, page 121.
2. Prof. I. Daniel Rupp, *Immigrants in Pennsylvania*, page 404; *Pennsylvania German Pioneers*, Volume 1, pages 744-745.
3. German Indentured Servants, records book available in the Historical Society of Pennsylvania, 1300 Locust Street, Philadelphia, Pennsylvania.
4. *Associators and Militia*, Pennsylvania Archives, Volume VIII, pages 554-556.
5. Rev. J.J. Kline Phd., *History of the Lutheran Church*, New Hanover, Pennsylvania, published 1910, pages 271, 573, 647.
6. *Ibid*, page 271.
7. St. Luke's Reformed Church, Trappe, Pennsylvania; 1840 U.S. Census Records, Skippack, Pennsylvania; 1850 U.S. Census Records, Schuylkill Township, Pennsylvania; and private family Bible.
8. 1840 U.S. Census Records, Skippack, Pennsylvania; 1850 U.S. Census Records, Schuylkill Township, Pennsylvania; 1860 U.S. Census

Records, Upper ProvidenceTownship, Pennsylvania; and private family Bible.

9. Chester County Historical Society, newspaper files, Chester, Pennsylvania; and private family Bible.

10. Private family Bible.

11. Copies of U.S. Government Pension Records and Army Discharge Records, in the author's possession.

12. 1860 U.S. Census Records, Port Providence, Pennsylvania; 1870 U.S. Census Records, Trappe, Pennsylvnia; 1880 U.S. Census Records, Phoenixville, Pennsylvnia; and private family Bible.

13. Whaling Ship records, *Mary & Helen,* California death certificate #30-028226; and author's correspondence and interviews.

14. Pinkerton Report dated April 23, 1902. Most Pinkerton files are handwritten copies of memos and letters which are often undated and unsigned. Because they are hand copies, some changes and/or errors were occasionally made from copy to copy. I have tried to be as exact as possible when using Pinkerton files for this reason.

15. Private family Bible; author's correspondence and interviews.

16. Emma Longabaugh's will, #48693, Montgomery County, Pennsylvania; author's correspondence and interviews.

17. Private family records; author's correspondence and interviews.

18. *Ibid.*

19. 1870 U.S. Census Records, Trappe, Pennsylvania; Montgomery County History, edited by Bean, local history available at *Montgomery County Library*, Norristown, Pennsylvania; and local history available at Trappe Historical Society, Trappe, Pennsylvania.

20. 1880 U.S. Census Records, West Vincent, Pennsylvnia; author's correspondence and interview with Ralston family.

21. Private family records.

22. *Ibid.*

23. Author's correspondence and interviews with descendants of George Longenbaugh.

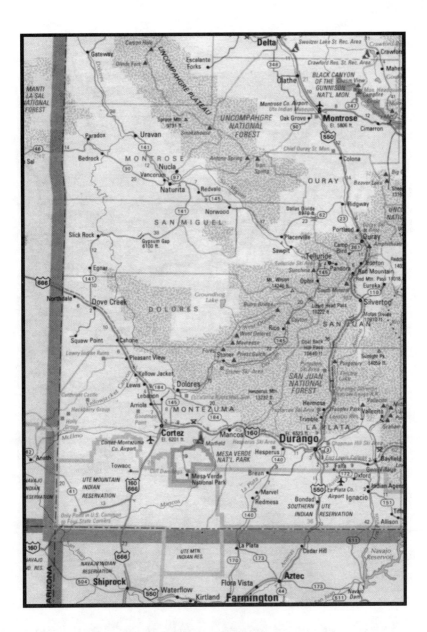

*Map of southwest Colorado and the
Four Corners area.*

The George Longenbaugh Family. (Courtesy of Harry and Frances Longenbaugh of Cortez, Colorado.)

Chapter Two

The Cortez Connection

By 1884, George Longenbaugh moved his family on to Cortez, Colorado, and Harry moved with them. George continued to raise horses and was an active board member with the Montezuma Valley Irrigation District in Cortez. Harry worked as a horse wrangler with Henry Goodman, the foreman for the LC Ranch.[1] In their spare time, George and Harry worked the family homestead. Harry stayed two more years with George, Mary and the boys. A special bond was formed between this family and Harry, and when Walter married and had a family of his own, he named his second son Harry.

In 1884, Cortez, Colorado was not yet an actual town. It was barely a tent city and was not founded until 1886.[2] As with many of the small rugged towns of the early west, it grew fast and wild. The area held a lot of potential for ranchers and cattleman, with the grass in nearby McElmo Canyon said to be as high as the stirrup of a saddle.[3]

With such inviting possibilities, the George Longenbaugh family decided to move from Durango to homestead at the future site of Cortez, about 48 miles away.[4] The area appealed to other families as well. The Maddens were in nearby Mancos, and the McCarty brothers moved to Cortez from the neighboring LaSal

Main Street in Cortez Colorado in the late 1890's or early 1900's. (Courtesy of Duane Neal.)

Mountains of Utah (their ranch was one mile from the Longenbaughs).[5] In later years Harry and Bill Madden robbed at least one train together.[6] By 1885 Robert LeRoy Parker (Butch Cassidy) and Willard Erastus Christiansen (Matt Warner) also lived in the area. In a manuscript credited to Butch Cassidy, he named Harry Longabaugh as being his first recruited outlaw pal.[7]

Young and impressionable, Harry was in the right place at the right time. Half a dozen future outlaw partners lived within a radius of about 75 miles, a one day's ride on horseback. George Longenbaugh raised horses. His cousin Harry became a horse wrangler. The ability to recognize and train good horses probably made Harry especially appealing to Butch, Matt and other gang members. The trade Harry learned when he came west served him well during his outlaw years. Relay horses were critical for a clean *getaway*.

Goodman, Harry's boss, was the foreman of the LC Ranch. The LC was owned by the Widow Lacy and

*Another view of Main Street, Cortez, Colorado.
(Courtesy of Duane Neal.)*

ran about 5000 head of cattle.[8] Their brand was an *L on
the right hip and a C on the right ribs, with a left ear
grubbed*, but rustlers found it quite easy to change it into
BOY.[9] Their cattle ranged from Montezuma County to
the open range in McElmo Canyon and on into the Blue
Mountains of Utah. The main range camp was just
beyond Goodmans Point, near Recapture Canyon, not
far from the Longenbaugh homestead.[10] Today what is
left of the old Longenbaugh homestead is located near
County Road L and Twenty-Third Street.

Researcher Pearl Baker told the story of a friendly
feud between Goodman's men and the hands of a neighboring ranch.[11] The Carlisle Ranch of Monticello, Utah
was a large cattle and sheep ranch, owned by a group of
Englishmen named Hudson and Carlisle.[12] Mr. Carlisle
ran the outfit with his foreman, Len Scott. One of the
ranch hands was Dan Parker, a younger brother of
Butch Cassidy.

25

Cowboy friends, from left, Henry Goodman, Gus Heffernon and Davy Crockett, in photo taken at Trinidad, Colorado. (Courtesy Chuck Hornung.)

Original building on Goodman's ranch.
(Courtesy Sundance Properties.)

While Carlisle and Scott were away on business one time, Dan Parker took advantage of their absence and butchered a number of sheep from the Goodman Ranch where young Harry Longabaugh was working. Goodman and Carlisle were business rivals. When Carlisle returned and saw the Goodman skins, he knew that Goodman would be angry if he saw them. So Carlisle had Scott hide the skins in an old cabin in Monticello. While changing for a local dance a few nights later, one of Goodman's men noticed the hides in the corner of the cabin.

The Goodman ranch hand loaded the hides on his horse to report the theft to Goodman. Parker saw what was going on and decided to protect himself. While Goodman's hand was inside the ranch house arguing with Scott, Parker switched the hides for some marked

The Cortez, Colorado relatives Harry and Frances Longenbaugh with the author's husband, Paul Ernst. (Courtesy Sundance Properties.)

with the Carlisle brand. The Goodman ranch hand then went to awaken Goodman and report the theft. They went outside to see the evidence and found Carlisle hides instead, and Goodman angrily ordered all the hides to be returned immediately.

Another well-known story was told of a horse race in McElmo Canyon.[13] Horse racing was a popular pastime, and one of the best horses around in 1889 was the mare Betty. Matt Warner and Tom McCarty traveled the area racing Betty and winning against all the local favorites. At a race in Telluride, Butch Cassidy (then a mining laborer) wagered his entire outfit and lost. However, Matt, Tom, and Butch hit it off quite well, and Butch joined the duo as a jockey and thus kept his belongings.

After winning races in Durango, Mancos, and Rico, they offered to race the one-eyed Indian pony White Face at McElmo Canyon in Cortez. Spectators came from miles around to watch and wager on the race. The Indians put up blankets and their horse to cover their bet. Betty won easily, but the Indians were reluctant to give White Face up in payment. Angry threats were exchanged, and McCarty began beating an Indian with his quirt. Warner and Cassidy held off the other Indians with their Winchesters, and they hightailed it to McCarty's cabin nearby. The next morning, Indians surrounded the cabin and attempted to reclaim White Face. A shot was fired from the cabin that left one Indian dead. While Winchesters were again leveled at the Indians, they collected their dead companion and left. Butch, Tom, and Matt also left before the Indians could return and headed through Cortez to Telluride.

Because of Harry's interest in horses, his cousin's reputation as a breeder of good horseflesh, and the close proximity of McElmo Canyon to Goodman's Point and Cortez, presumably Harry either watched or knew of this race. This was one of the many opportunities for Harry to meet the men with whom he would later ride. He was easily recruited because of his independent and carefree spirit and his desire to see and do more than Cortez had to offer. The outlaws saw a young man with a fast draw.

Notes

1. Author's correspondence and interviews with descendants of George Longenbaugh; Ira S. Freeman, *A History of Montezuma County,* Colorado, published 1958, Johnson Publishing Company, Boulder, Colorado, page 55.
2. June Head, editor, *Our One Hundred Years of Banking in Montezuma County,* First National Bank, Cortez, Colorado, published 1986, Beaber Printing Company, Cortez, Colorado, page 21.
3. Freeman, op cit, page 55 and 57.
4. Private family records.
5. Author's correspondence and interviews with descendants of George

Longenbaugh; Tom McCarty, *Tom McCarty's Own Story*, published 1986, Rocky Mountain House Press, Hamilton, Montana, pages 1, 28, and 54; Charles Kelly, *The Outlaw Trail, The Story of Butch Cassidy and the Wild Bunch*, published 1959, Bonanza Books, New York, pages 30-32.

6. Malta, Montana, train robbery, November 29, 1892; J.D.B. Greig memo to Pinkertons dated June 24, unknown year.

7. Larry Pointer, *In Search of Butch Cassidy*, published 1977, University of Oklahoma Press, page 98. While obviously not Butch, the manuscript author was apparently someone who had much inside information available.

8. Freeman, op cit, page 55; Perkins, Nielson, and Jones, *Saga of San Juan*, published 1957, San Juan County Daughters of Utah Pioneers, page 133; Fern D. Ellis, *Come Back to My Valley*, page 89.

9. George W. Menefee, *Cow Talk*, memoirs recorded by Lottie W. Reddert.

10. Perkins, Nielson, and Jones, op cit, page 133.

11. Pearl Baker, *The Wild Bunch at Robbers Roost*, published 1971, Abelard-Schuman, New York, page 110-113.

12. Wilma Crisp Bankston, *Where Eagles Winter*, as quoted in author's correspondence with June Head on 11-25-88.

13. Baker, op cit, page 57-58; Lula Parker Betenson, *Butch Cassidy My Brother*, published 1984, Brigham Young University Press, pages 59-60; Matt Warner, *The Last of the Bandit Riders*, published 1950, Bonanza Books, New York, pages 110 -116.

THE EARLY WEST

Henry F. Niedringhaus.

P. O. Address, 2nd and Cass Ave., St. Louis, Mo.

Edgar H. Niedringhaus, Foreman. Address, Blackmon, Mont.
Range, Hungry Creek.

Earmark

Other brands on cattle,

Other brands for horses,

 right hip

 or $\frac{N}{N}$ left ribs cattle
left thigh horses

N-N ads showing brands used by the Niedringhaus brothers.
(Courtesy Montana Historical Society.)

31

MONTANA STOCK GROWERS' ASSOCIATION

T. H. LOGAN, Manager, Miles City, Mont.

HOME LAND & CATTLE CO.
St. Louis, Mo.

P. O. Address, Miles City, Mont.

Range, on Big and Little Dry and Tributaries, and North side of Yellowstone.

Other brands on Cattle, left hip and side.

Other brands on Horses, on left hip.

N-N ads showing brands used by the Niedringhaus brothers. (Courtesy Montana Historical Society.)

Chapter Three

The N Bar N Ranch

I have always worked for an honest living; was employed last summer by one of the best outfits in Montana and don't think they can say aught against me.[1]

With the severe winter of 1884 and then the drought of 1886, Colorado's cattle ranches fell on hard times.[2] Some ranchers turned to cattle rustling, some sold out to larger foreign-owned outfits, and others sought new careers. Harry was again without work, but now he had a trade to follow. He hoped to find work with horses in a rodeo, according to family sources, and therefore headed north to find a job.[3]

About the same time, the N Bar N (N-N) outfit was trailing a large cattle drive along the same route, heading for Montana from Texas.[4] Harry signed on and worked his way north. Owners F.G. and William Neidringhaus were impressed enough to keep young Harry employed when the drive ended. However, he was laid off after winter began. The winter of 1886 to 1887 was extremely harsh, and the N Bar N lost 20,000 head of cattle.[5]

The Neidringhaus brothers, originally from St. Louis, Missouri, had made their fortune in enamelware as owners of the National Enameling and Stamping Mills.[6] F.G. became president of their cattle concerns,

Photo of N-N Ranch Winter Camp on the Yellowstone. (Courtesy Montana Historical Society.)

and William remained president of the enamelware company. In 1884 the brothers established the N Bar N with 6,000 head of cattle, which they acquired as payment for a bad debt.[7] Their first cattle drive in the fall of 1884 was so successful that they built a ranch on the Little Dry Creek near Wolf Point, Montana. The N Bar N had cattle on the open range as well, running from Wolf Point and Rock Creek to Miles City.[8] It was the largest ranch in Valley County, Montana by the late 1880's.[9]

The ranch's main office was at Cass Avenue and Second Street in St. Louis, and Miles City, Montana was the range address.[10] They began with one ranch on the Little Dry and then added a second ranch on Rock Creek with many camp ranches in between. They used the HL and N Bar N brands for cattle and horses.[11] The HL brand stood for the Home Land and Cattle Company, the full name for the Neidringhaus concerns. At their peak,

*N-N Ranch at Prairie Elk. (Courtesy
Montana Historical Society.)*

the N Bar N ran 50,000 head of cattle and employed 150 people.[12]

It is interesting that.. *during 1886 the Curry boys had cut a deal with the 60,000 acre Marlowe and MacNamara (sic) outfit near Big Sandy to handle their horses on a share basis.*[13] This is likely where Sundance and Harvey Logan began working together.

In 1895, the N Bar N headquarters moved to Oswego, Montana. Harry Longabaugh was again working for them as one of the 50 ranch hands listed at that time.[14] In 1897 the Neidringhaus brothers sold their ranch to McNamaro and Marlow of Great Falls, Montana who were ranchers at neighboring Rock Creek. F.G. Neidringhaus then bought a smaller ranch in the area and continued using the N Bar N brand.[15]

One of Sundance's fellow ranch hands at the N Bar N during 1895 had been *Dutch Henry* Ieuch.[16] After the N Bar N was sold in 1897, Dutch Henry headed a small gang of rustlers headquartered just north of Culbertson, Montana and he occasionally used the Hole In The Wall hideout in Wyoming.[17] Sundance was a member of this gang.

Dutch Henry's gang rustled together with another band of outlaws known as the Nelson - Jones Gang. The head of that gang was a man named Frank Jones.[18] This Frank Jones must have made a big impression on Sundance, because Sundance often borrowed his name as an alias in later years. The real Frank Jones died under mysterious circumstances near Culbertson.

In June of 1900, an informant from Malta, Montana, wrote the Pinkertons about a number of outlaws living near Culbertson, Montana.[19] He wrote . . . *About Culbertson there are a couple of fellows, ex-cowboys . . . formerly worked for the N - N outfit that are outlaws and fugitives from justice. There is another party named Logenbough (sic) who was supposed to have been implicated in the holdup which occurred at Malta a number of years ago. Some people here think he is one of the Jones or Roberts boys . . . I would like to see Valley County rid of this class of her population. They rustle cattle and horses, do many misdeeds and either hide in Canada or across the border.* The informant, J.D.B. Grieg, was the editor of the *Harlem Enterprise* and also knew the Curry boys, although he claimed not to know of their illegal activities.[20]

Culbertson is located at the intersection of Routes 2 and 16, about 175 miles east of Malta, Montana. Today it's residents are descendants of pioneering ranchers. The town recently celebrated its centennial and published a book for the occasion. *100 Years in Culbertson*, mentions both Sundance and Harvey Logan (Kid Curry), as well as the local rustlers.[21] Sundance's loyalties to the N Bar N and Culbertson could be the reason that he only participated in one Montana robbery.

In the early 1900's Dutch Henry went to South America for a while.[22] He may have visited his old friend Sundance on the ranch in Cholila, Argentina. Dutch Henry returned to Montana and was eventually killed by the Canadian Mounted Police.

Notes

1. *Daily Yellowstone Journal* (Miles City), June 9, 1887.
2. Freeman, op cit, page 52; author's correspondence and interviews with descendants of George Longenbaugh and with June Head.
3. *Ibid.*
4. A.W.Neidringhaus, unpublished collection of Livestock History, Montana Historical Society, Helena, Montana.
5. Unpublished collection of Livestock History, Montana Historical Society, Helena, Montana.
6. Charles F. Campbell, unpublished collection of Livestock History, Montana Historical Society, Helena, Montana.
7. Neidringhaus, op cit.
8. Mark H. Brown and W.R. Felton, *Before Barbed Wire*, published 1956, Bramhall House, New York, end paper map.
9. *From Buffalo Bones to Sonic Boom*, a publication of the Glasgow Jubilee Committee, July 1962, page 5.
10. N-N advertisements in *The Weekly Yellowstone Journal* and *The Live Stock Reporter*.
11. *Brand Book of the Montana Stock Growers Association for 1885 and 1886*, published by Montana Stock Growers Association, pages 16 and 91; *Van Dersal & Connor's Stockgrowers Directory of Marks and Brands*, published by Van Dersal & Connor, Helena, Montana, page 123.
12. Neidringhaus, op cit.
13. Alan Lee Brekke, *Kid Curry: Train Robber*, published 1989, *Harlem News/Chinook Opinion*, page 10, F. Bruce Lamb, *Kid Curry, The Life and Times of Harvey Logan and the Wild Bunch*, published 1991, Johnson Books, page 209.
14. *From Buffalo Bones to Sonic Boom*, op cit, page 6.
15. Neidringhaus, op cit.
16. *From Buffalo Bones to Sonic Boom*, op cit, page 6, Loretta Segars, *100 Years in Culbertson*, published 1986, Culbertson Centennial Steering Committee, page 127.
17. Kelly, op cit, page 109.
18. Segars, op cit, page 127.
19. J.D.B. Greig letter to Pinkerton Detective Agency, June 15, 1900.
20. Brekke, op cit, pages 50, 52 and 56.
21. Segars, op cit, pages 42, 84-5, and 127.
22. *Ibid*, page 127.

Indictment #33. (Courtesy Crook County Museum, Sundance, Wyoming.)

Chapter Four

Alias the Sundance Kid

Having got discharged last winter I went to the Black Hills to seek employment.[1]

Harry went to the Black Hills area, near the Montana - Wyoming - South Dakota border, but he could not find ranch work. He was only able to earn his room and board. After about a month and a half, he worked his way back towards Montana, via the VVV (Three V) Ranch in Sundance, Wyoming. The town of Sundance today lies just off Interstate 90, truly in the middle of nowhere, just as it was 100 years ago.

The VVV Ranch, also known as Western Ranches, Ltd., was located on the Belle Fourche River just north of Sundance. Their horse camp and winter quarters were located on Crow Creek near the tri-state border. The old camp area is still a ranch today, and the original cabin is now used as a community building.[2]

In 1887 the VVV Ranch was owned by English investors and was under the management of John Clay and his assistant, Robert Robinson. John Clay was a very influential man in the area.[3] He was president of the Wyoming Stock Growers Association and a member of the exclusive Cheyenne Club. In later years he and

39

*A bird's eye view of Sundance, Wyoming.
(Courtesy Wyoming State Archives.)*

Robinson became major stockholders in the Butte County
Bank in Belle Fourche, South Dakota.

On February 27, 1887, young Harry stole a light
grey horse, a revolver, and a saddle outfit from Alonzo
Craven of the VVV Ranch and headed up toward Miles
City, Montana.[4] Clay had the employees of the VVV
Ranch spread out over the area in search of a *smooth-
faced, grey-eyed boy* and the stolen goods.[5] It was not
until March 15, 1887 that James Wedner of the VVV
Ranch finally rode into Sundance, the Crook County
seat, to file charges with Sheriff James Ryan.

Ryan then picked up Harry's trail to Miles City.
By April 8, 1887, Ryan had arrested Harry but did not
immediately leave Miles City. Harry was housed in the
small jail located on the north side of the new courthouse
at Main and Seventh Streets until April 12th.[6] For

Sundance, Wyoming street scene.
(Courtesy Wyoming State Archives.)

reasons unknown, Ryan and young Harry then boarded the Northern Pacific Railroad to St. Paul, Minnesota, nearly 700 miles away; and then the Fremont, Elkhorn and Missouri Valley train to Rapid City, South Dakota. Somewhere near Duluth, Minnesota, Harry and an accomplice picked the locks of his shackles and handcuffs and jumped off the moving train while Ryan was in the bathroom.[7] Some researchers believe Butch Cassidy was in the Miles City area at this time, having come up from Wyoming about 1886.[8] Because of their earlier acquaintance in Colorado, Butch and Harry might have sought one another out, and Butch may have acted as Harry's accomplice. Sheriff Ryan offered a $250 reward, but Harry had escaped. Foolishly, he returned to the Miles City area.

Deputy Sheriff Eph K. Davis and Stock Inspector W. Smith caught up with young Harry near the N Bar

Ranch on the Powder River outside Miles City.[9] (The N
Bar was a neighboring ranch to the N Bar N. Harry had
worked at both ranches.[10]) Harry was again shackled
and handcuffed, and Davis and Smith were left to guard
him in the Custer County jail. Smith fell asleep, and
Davis pretended to do the same. Harry again picked his
locks and made for the windows to escape, but Davis
pulled out his gun and stopped him. By morning, Sheriff
Tom Irvine had telegraphed Ryan to come pick up his
prisoner. Irvine also put in a claim for the reward money.
In May, 1888, the Crook County, Wyoming, Com-
missioner's meeting refused to pay the reward to either
Ryan or Irvine.

On June 7, 1887, the *Daily Yellowstone Journal*
published a front-page article detailing Harry's arrest
and attempted escape.[11] It also listed a few small, local
robberies, giving *the Kid* the credit for them. The article
then compared Harry's exploits with the James boys.

Harry wrote back to the paper. This is our one
firsthand glimpse into the evolving Sundance Kid, who
at age twenty still had choices. On June 9th, the *Daily
Yellowstone Journal* published his reply.[12]

*In your issue of the 7th inst. I read a very sensa-
tional and partly untrue article, which places me
before the public not even second to the notorious
Jesse James. Admitting that I have done wrong
and expecting to be dealt with according to law
and not by false reports from parties who should
blush with shame to make them, I ask a little of
your space to set my case before the public in a true
light. In the first place I have always worked for
an honest living; was employed last summer by
one of the best outfits in Montana and don't think
they can say aught against me, but having got
discharged last winter I went to the Black Hills to*

seek employment — which I could not get — and was forced to work for my board a month and a half, rather than to beg or steal. I finally started back to the vicinity of Miles City, as it was spring, to get employment on the range and was arrested at the above named place and charged with having stolen a horse at Sundance, where I was being taken by Sheriff Ryan, whom I escaped from by jumping from the cars, which I judged were running at the rate of 100 miles an hour.

After this my course of outlawry commenced, and I suffered terribly for the want of food in the hope of getting back south without being detected, where I would be looked upon as I always had been, and not as a criminal. Contrary to the statement in the Journal, I deny having stolen any horses in Canada and selling them near Benton, or anyplace else, up to the time I was captured, at which time I was riding a horse which I bought and paid for, nor had I the slightest idea of stealing any horses. I am aware that some of your readers will say my statement should be taken for what it is worth, on account of the hard name which has been forced upon me, nevertheless it is true. As for my recapture by Deputy Sheriff Davis, all I can say is that he did his work well and were it not for his 'playing possum' I would now be on my way south, where I had hoped to go and live a better life. HARRY LONGABAUGH

Sheriff Ryan arrived in Miles City on June 19th to take possession of the prisoner.[13] This time when they left for Sundance, they took a buckboard and followed the Miles City to Deadwood stage coach road, arriving three days later.[14] Harry was placed in the new jail in

Miles City, Montana. Main Street looking east, July 1884. (L.A. Huffman photograph, Courtesy Montana Historical Society.)

Sundance, and held on Grand Larceny charges.[15] The court records show that he gave his home state as Pennsylvania, his occupation as cowboy, his height as six feet, and his age as 26. (As Harry was only 20, I suspect that the court clerk wrote a sloppy and often misread zero.) The records also show that he had no parents. His mother, Annie, died in May, 1887, but his father, Josiah, was still alive. This may have been to protect them, or he may have felt that part of his life was over. Harry continued his attempts to escape, but failed in each try.[16]

Court was not in session until August 2, 1887, so Harry was finally indicted on August 3rd on three counts of Grand Larceny. The prosecuting attorney in the case was Benjamin F. Fowler who became U.S. Attorney for Wyoming from 1890 to 1894 and then state attorney general from 1895 to 1898. On August 4th, the court appointed Joseph Stotts to represent young Harry, who could not afford his own attorney. Stotts later was elected as a Republican to the state legislature. The next day, August 5th, Harry pleaded not guilty. However, Stotts apparently convinced Harry to plead guilty to horse stealing, indictment #33, in exchange for the other two indictments being dropped. Harry was immediately sentenced by Judge William L. Maginnis to 18 months at hard labor. However, Harry was confined to the Sundance jail rather than being transferred to the penitentiary at Laramie, Wyoming because he was under 21.

Harry continued his escape attempts and nearly succeeded on Tuesday, May 1, 1888. When Jailor Daley took dinner into the cell around 6 p.m., Harry and fellow prisoner Jim O'Connor assaulted him. O'Connor was able to escape for a few hours but Daley overpowered Harry.[17] In January, 1889, H.A. Alden, a new Crook County prosecutor, wrote to Governor Thomas Moonlight, asking for a pardon for Harry. On February 4, 1889, one day before his scheduled release, Harry was granted a full pardon. The governor wrote, *He is still under 21 years of age, and his behavior has been good since confinement, showing an earnest desire to reform.*[18] Because of the element of time, however, it is not known whether Harry was ever notified of his pardon.

The Sundance Gazette wrote on February 8, 1889, *The term of 'Kid' Longabaugh expired on Tuesday morning, and the young man at once hired himself to the Hills, taking the coach for Deadwood.*[19] Harry was not heard from again until May 17, 1889, when the *Sundance Gazette* told of the Buck Hanby shooting.[20] Hanby was wanted for a murder in Nebraska and was hiding in a dugout on Oil Creek, about 35 miles north of Sundance. With him were three other men, including Harry, who was then going by the alias of *Kid Chicago*.[21] When Sheriff E.B. Armstrong and Deputy Sheriff James Swisher burst in, they caught Hanby unarmed. Hanby

Governor's Pardon for Harry A. Longabaugh 1889,
Secretary of State Record of Pardons, Volume 1.
(Courtesy Crook County, Wyoming court records.)

reached for his gun and was killed at close range. After questioning, the others were released. On May 18th, Swisher swore out a complaint against Harry, because he feared retaliation for Hanby's killing. The warrant was filed on May 24th, and showed that Sheriff J.W. Rogers had arrested Harry. However, there is no record that the case was ever heard.[22]

Harry A. Longabaugh became the *Kid* from Sundance.

Notes

1. *Daily Yellowstone Journal* (Miles City), June 9, 1887.
2. Mary Garman, "Harry Longabaugh - The Sundance Kid, The Early Years, 1867-1889," *Bits and Pieces*, February 1977, page 6, author's interviews with Mary Garman.
3. *Ibid*; Edward M. Kirby, *The Rise & Fall of the Sundance Kid*, published 1983, Western Publications, Iola, Wisconsin, page 31.
4. *The Sundance Gazette*, March 18, 1887.
5. *The Sundance Gazette*, March 18, 1887.
6. *Centennial Roundup*, published 1987, The Miles City Star, pg. 43.
7. *The Sundance Gazette*, April 22, 1887.
8. Pointer, op cit, page 48; Richard Patterson, *Historical Atlas of the Outlaw West*, published 1985, Johnson Books, Boulder, Colorado, page 98.
9. Garman, op cit, page 3.
10. Kirby, op cit.
11. *Daily Yellowstone Journal*, June 7, 1887.
12. *Ibid*, June 9, 1887.
13. *The Sundance Gazette*, June 24, 1887.
14. *Ibid*.
15. Garman, op cit, page 4; Crook County (Wyoming) Court Records.
16. *The Sundance Gazette*, July 22, 1887.
17. *Ibid*, May 4, 1888.
18. Garman, op cit, page 5, Crook County (Wyoming) Court Records; copy of Pardon in author's possession.
19. *The Sundance Gazette*, February 8, 1889.
20. *Ibid*, May 17, 1889.
21. Arrest Warrant, Crook County (Wyoming) Court Records.
22. *Ibid*; Garman, op cit, page 6.

Tom McCarty. (Courtesy Jim Dullenty)

Chapter Five

Telluride

June 24, 1889

Because communication and transportation were much slower in the 1800's, proper identification and capture were the exception, not the rule. The members of the Wild Bunch were often credited with any unsolved area crimes, occasionally without any proof. Conversely, they were also often overlooked, in spite of prevailing evidence.

Telluride was an old mining camp tucked into a corner of the San Juan Mountains of the San Miguel Valley. Originally named Columbia, the town was one of the oldest in the state. It was changed to Telluride probably for tellurium, a by-product of the area mines. Oldtimers often said that it actually was *to hell you ride*. In either case, it was a rough, bustling, frontier town.

Today Telluride, Colorado is a ski resort located at the end of State Highway 145. The entire town is a museum with many of the old, original buildings. New structures are built to blend in with the flavor of an 1880's mining town. While the San Miguel Valley Bank no longer exists, the town looks much as it did 100 years ago. (The bank was on the left-hand side of Main Street going into town.)

Butch Cassidy had worked on and off in the mines for a number of years. He and Matt Warner both worked

Near Tom McCarty's hideout in Cortez, Colorado.
(Courtesy Sundance Properties.)

for a local rancher named Harry B. Adsit in nearby Lone Cone.[1] Therefore, Butch, Matt Warner and Tom McCarty, whose cabin was 75 miles away in Cortez (near the George Longenbaugh homestead), all had knowledge of the town, the area, and the bank. The three possibly felt the robbery would be an easy one. The gold ore mined in the area promised that it would be a rich one.

On Monday morning, June 24, 1889, Butch, Matt and Tom dressed up as dude cowboys and slowly rode into town and casually surveyed the town.[2] They knew ahead of time that the town marshal Jim Clark was not around. (In fact, Clark is said to have later bragged about receiving a $2200 payoff for being out of town.) The three arrived in front of the bank around the noontime break, when little was happening.[3]

The county clerk, Charles Painter, left the bank just before the men pulled up. Teller C. Hyde was alone behind the counter, with a pile of money in front of him. Tom stayed outside with the horses while Butch and

McCarty's hideout was a mile and a half southwest of the Longenbaugh ranch. (Courtesy Sundance Prop.)

Matt went inside. While Matt covered Hyde, Butch filled a sack with the money on the counter. Butch then collected the money inside the vault. Totals vary from $10,500 to $30,000, but newspaper accounts at the time said they got about $20,750.[4]

As the gang raced out of town toward their hideout in the Mancos Mountains 35 miles away, they unexpectedly ran into Adsit. He recognized Butch and Matt as they raced past him. From that point on, they were known as professional outlaws.

Horse relays were set up along the path of escape to enable them to stay well ahead of any posse. Depending upon which source is used, the names and number of relay holders differ.[5] Suggested names are Kid Madden, Bill and/or Bert Madden (brothers from Mancos), Bert Charter, Kid Brown, and Dan Parker (a younger brother of Butch Cassidy). All these names were of young men living around the Cortez area.

*Main Street, Telluride, Colorado today.
(Courtesy Sundance Properties.)*

As the thieves raced towards Keystone Hill and their first relay, a posse headed by Sheriffs James A. Beattie and J.C. Love got too close for comfort. One of the gang tied a tree limb onto the tail of a relay horse and sent it running back down the mountain. The noise and confusion caused the posse to back off, allowing the outlaws enough time to escape.

Three days after the Telluride robbery, on June 27th, the *Rocky Mountain News* wrote an article that suggested that there were four robbers, not three:

> *The robbery of the San Miguel Valley Bank of Telluride on Monday by four daring cowboys . . . the four rode over to the bank, and leaving their horses in charge of one of the number, two remained on the sidewalk and the fourth entered the bank.*[6]

San Miguel Valley Bank, Telluride, Colorado.

Robbed June 10, 1889 by Butch Cassidy and his gang. Butch and his cohorts were known as "the wild Bunch." James A. Beattie, sheriff of San Miguel County was joined by J.C. Love, sheriff of Montezuma County in the investigation that followed.

San Miguel County records show $885.07 was spent on man-hire and horse rentals during the man-hunt. Although records are confusing and do not always agree on account of the robbery is interesting reading as told by Wilson Rockwell and is available in his books at your local library.

Hope this answers your question at least in part. Kind regards.

C.M. Engel

Text of the letter of corroboration sent to Walter Longenbaugh concerning the Telluride robbery. (Courtesy Harry and Frances Longenbaugh.)

Pearl Baker's research turned up an eyewitness to a train robbery near Dolores a few weeks after the Telluride bank job.[7] Roy Dickerson, in recounting his story, said, *There were four of the fellows that had robbed the bank at Telluride*. So there were at least two reports of four robbers, rather than three, and both were given shortly after the actual robbery. Even Tom McCarty said in his autobiography, *two of my partners* which implied that he had more than two partners.[8]

Sundance was released from prison a month before the robbery. By the end of May, 1889, Sundance had left the Wyoming area and was headed for Cortez and George Longenbaugh's ranch 75 miles from Telluride. *Tom McCarty's Ranch was a mile and a half southwest of George Longenbaugh's homestead in the sagebrush and cedars.*[9] One thing George Longenbaugh's son Walter remembered and passed on to his family was

Matt Warner in 1937, the year before his death.

that the family knew young Harry had helped to rob the bank in Telluride.[10] After Walter's death, the family found a letter from a well-known, local historian (also deceased) about the Telluride bank robbery in answer to a letter from Walter. He had apparently written to gain corroboration for Sundance's participation in the Telluride robbery. In it the historian stated *records are confusing and do not always agree.*

Family history also includes that George's wife Mary provided provisions when the young gang was hiding out at Tom McCarty's ranch.[11]

The two eyewitness accounts, the evidence listed in the newspapers of the time, and the account by Walter Longenbaugh lead one to believe that Telluride can be added to the list of robberies in which Sundance participated.

Notes

1. Bankston, op cit, page 45; Betenson, op cit, page 62.
2. Kenneth Jessen, *Colorado Gunsmoke*, page 247; Pointer, op cit, page 52.
3. *Ibid.*
4. *Rocky Mountain News*, June 27, 1889.
5. Baker, op cit, pages 159-160; Warner, op cit, pages 117-123.
6. *Rocky Mountain News*, June 27, 1889; Pointer, op cit, page 51, Kelly, op cit, pages 29-32.
7. Baker, op cit, page 161-163.
8. McCarty, op cit, page 29.
9. Author's correspondence and interviews with relatives of George Longenbaugh.
10. Author's correspondence and interviews with descendants of George Longenbaugh; copy of 1971 C.M. Engel letter in author's possession.
11. Author's correspondence and interviews with descendants of George Longenbaugh; McCarty, op cit, pages 1, 26-28, and 54; E. Richard Churchill, *They Rode With Butch Cassidy, The McCartys*, page 16.

Annie Rogers & Kid Curry (Harvey Logan). (Courtesy Jim Dullenty.)

Chapter Six

The Wild Bunch

The Wild Bunch was a loosely-knit band of outlaws with a constantly changing membership. During their relatively short period of notoriety in the 1880's and 90's, there were probably fewer than thirty men actually within the ranks of the group. Three or four would join together for a job and drift apart. Another half dozen would come together and separate. The reason for this was to avoid being trailed after a job. Each member would head for a different hideout and lose the posse along the way. Since each robbery was perpetrated by a slightly different group, there was constant confusion about the actual size of the Wild Bunch.

An inner circle developed under the leadership of Butch Cassidy, and Sundance was a member of this core group. Butch was born Robert Leroy Parker on April 13, 1866, in Beaver, Utah. He was the eldest of a large, Mormon, farming family.[1] Early in his life, he came under the influence of Mike Cassidy, a ranch hand and occasional cattle rustler. Butch was an apt pupil and apparently admired Cassidy so much that he eventually adopted his name.[2] The nickname Butch was earned when he worked as a butcher near Rock Springs, Wyoming.[3] It is said that Butch was a true gentleman in spite of his chosen avocation.

Elzy Lay. (Courtesy Jim Dullenty.)

The man with the wildest reputation was Harvey Logan, alias Kid Curry. Logan once had a small ranch in Landusky, Montana with some of his cousins.[4] His cousins included Lonnie, Johnny, and Henry Logan, and Bob Lee; all small-time outlaws. However, after killing two prominent townsmen, Pike Landusky and W.H. Jim Winters, Logan left the area.[5] He carried his reputation as a cold-blooded killer with him. The Pinkerton reports suggest that he would just as soon have killed you as look at you.[6] Nearly all of the shootings involving the Wild Bunch were credited to him.

Although eventually arrested and jailed in Knoxville, Tennessee, Logan escaped. On June 7, 1904, after robbing the Denver and Rio Grande Railroad near Parachute, Colorado, Logan supposedly committed suicide as a posse trapped him in a canyon near Rifle, Colorado.[7] However, the Pinkertons included him on a wanted poster which they circulated in South America, and rumors about him persisted for years.[8]

Flatnose George Sutherland Currie was born in Canada on March 20, 1871.[9] His nickname was the result of a flattened bridge from a broken nose. In the beginning, Flatnose probably carried more authority than Butch did when in the Hole In The Wall area, where Flatnose had a small ranch. However, he was a bit too reckless for some of the experienced outlaws. Flatnose was killed on April 17, 1900 while being pursued by Sheriffs William Preece and Jesse M. Tyler for cattle rustling.[10]

William Ellsworth *Elzy* Lay, born November 25, 1868, was undoubtedly the mildest of the Wild Bunch. He was married to Maude Davis, and they had a daughter, Marvel.[11] After Elzy was released from the New Mexico Penitentiary, he settled down with his second wife, had a family, and lived a very productive life. He died in Los Angeles, California, in 1933.[12]

Butch Cassidy, the Sundance Kid's best friend and partner in crime. (Courtesy Jim Dullenty.)

These were the best known of the Wild Bunch, but many others were among the larger membership. Ben Kilpatrick, alias the Tall Texan, was from a Texas family that laid claim to a number of lesser-known outlaws. He and his girlfriend, Laura Bullion, participated in a number of robberies in the last year or two that the Wild Bunch was active. He was arrested in St. Louis, Missouri and was sent to prison in Atlanta, Georgia for 15 years. He was killed March 13, 1912 while robbing the Southern Pacific train near Sanderson, Texas.[13]

Bill Carver, alias G.W. Franks, was another of the later arrivals to the Bunch. Carver married Lillie Davis, one of Fannie Porter's girls, during a visit to Fort Worth, Texas. He was killed on April 2, 1901, by Sheriff E.S. Bryant, in Sonora, Texas.[14]

Although never involved with the Wild Bunch, Matt Warner and Tom McCarty certainly were a part of Sundance's life. Matt Warner, born Willard Erastus Christiansen, served time in Utah for murder. Once released, he went straight and worked as a peace officer in Price, Utah. Matt died in 1938 leaving a wife and three children.[15]

Tom McCarty dropped out of sight after the Delta, Colorado bank robbery in which his brother and nephew were killed. Tom escaped and was rumored to have moved to Rosebud County, Montana.[16] Both Tom and Matt Warner penned autobiographies, which have been very helpful to researchers over the years.

The Wild Bunch members were often erroneously credited with unsolved bank and railroad robberies. Sundance was also blamed for several robberies he did not commit, as well as being thought innocent for some in which he might have participated.

One of these robberies was the Great Northern Railroad. It was held up about 2 p.m. outside Wagner,

Montana on July 3, 1901.[17] The thieves made off with approximately $40,000 in unsigned bank notes. Immediately after the robbery the posses began looking for Butch and Sundance. In fact, the Pinkertons prepared a wanted poster, Circular #2, although it was not actually released until January 24, 1902.[18] The poster was issued listing Sundance as a participant in the Great Northern Train Robbery.

Later in 1902 the Pinkertons discovered that Sundance sailed for Argentina on February 21, 1901, making Sundance's participation impossible.

In the middle of November, 1901, Ben Kilpatrick, alias the Tall Texan, and his girlfriend, Laura Bullion, were arrested in St. Louis.[19] They were carrying some of the forged bank notes from the Wagner robbery at the time of their arrest. When questioned by Chief of Detectives Desmond, Bullion reportedly identified her companion as Harry Longabaugh.[20] On November 15, 1901, the *Butte Inter-Mountain* carried the story of Sundance's capture. Bullion's incorrect identification was soon realized, and she and Kilpatrick were both tried and sent to prison.

Larry Pointer's book, *In Search of Butch Cassidy*, uses the manuscript credited to Butch Cassidy. It included two robberies in the area of Cortez, Colorado.[21] One remains unidentified, but the other was a Rio Grande Southern Flyer #6 robbery in Rico, Colorado. Rico was only 50 miles from the Longenbaugh home in Cortez and nothing conflicted with Sundance being there around July 6, 1898.

Pointer's book includes another robbery which remains unclear. It was a bank job in central or southern Utah in early 1896.[22] According to the manuscript, it was done by Butch and Sundance alone, and it resulted in a take of about $7,000. Again, the date is possible, and the geographical location is near both the Robbers Roost

Kid Curry. (Courtesy Jim Dullenty.)

hideout and *home* in Cortez. This robbery could have been the Castle Gate, Utah robbery.[23]

The Pleasant Valley Coal Company payroll, worth about $7,000, was stolen on April 21, 1897, by Butch Cassidy and Elzy Lay. Joe Walker was said to have held the relay and cut the telegraph wires. This robbery again fit the pattern of the right time and place categories, but there were two other convincing reasons. First, the Castle Gate description bore an uncanny resemblance to the unidentified robbery in central Utah as described above from Pointer's manuscript. Second, Castle Gate was the hometown of a large family named Thayne.[24] According to researcher Pearl Baker and the

Wagner Train Robbery, Express Car.

man known as Harry Longabaugh, Jr., Sundance was said to have been married to an Anna Marie Thayne, and Castle Gate has been rumored to have been her home town. Having family there would have made knowledge of the town and payroll easy to obtain and protection would also have been available.

The Pinkerton files include two newspaper articles regarding a New Mexico bank robbery in 1893. However, no further information has been located on this robbery.[25]

Notes

1. Betenson, op cit, page 32.
2. *Ibid*, page 64.
3. *Ibid*, page 72.
4. Kirby, op cit, pages 40 and 44.
5. *Ibid*; Horan, op cit, page 249; Kelly, op cit, page 267.
6. Pinkerton, op cit.
7. *Ibid*; Horan, op cit, page 249; Kelly, op cit, page 267.
8. Pinkerton, op cit, Spanish Wanted Circular, February 4, 1907.
9. Pointer, op cit, page 68.
10. Kelly, op cit, page 307.
11. *Ibid*, page 309; Baker, op cit, page 59.
12. Kelly, op cit, page 309.
13. *Ibid*, page 307.
14. *Ibid*.
15. *Ibid*, page 310; Warner, op cit.
16. Kelly, op cit, page 308; McCarty, op cit.
17. James D. Horan and Paul Sann, *Pictorial History of the Wild West*, Crown Publishers Inc., New York, pages 218-219.
18. *Ibid*; Pinkerton Detective Agency Records, owned by CPP in Van Nuys, California. Most Pinkerton files are handwritten copies of memos and letters which are often undated and unsigned. As they are hand copies, occasionally some changes and/or errors were made from copy to copy, so I tried to be as exact as possible when using them.
19. Horan and Sann, op cit, pages 218-219; Pointer, op cit, page 270.
20. Horan and Sann, op cit, page 223; *St. Louis Post Dispatch* as quoted by James D. Horan, *The Outlaws*, page 260.
21. Pointer, op cit, pages 256 and 276; *Denver Times*, July 6, 1898.
22. Pointer, op cit, page 103.
23. Kirby, op cit, page 55; Kouris, op cit, page 85.
24. Baker, op cit, pages 48 and 199; Harry Longabaugh Jr., lecture in Ogden, Utah, as quoted in *The Sun Advocate*, July 23, 1970.
25. Pinkerton, op cit.

Chapter Seven

The Outlaw Trail

The winding, roaming cattle trail known as the Owlhoot or Outlaw Trail ran in an imaginary line from Montana's open ranges down to New Mexico's ranches. Spaced along this trail were three well-known but remote outlaw hideouts: The Hole-In-The-Wall, Brown's Park, and Robbers Roost. To outlaws on the run, looking for their next job or just resting up over the winter, these were safe places because there would be no questions asked.

The Hole-In-The-Wall was the northern-most hideout located about 16 miles from the town of Kaycee. The town was named for the old KC Ranch in Wyoming. This ranch was the location of the final fight in the Johnson County War, a conflict between the small cattle ranchers and homesteaders and the foreign-owned cattle companies.[1] Hideout cabins were scattered about the area although there was no actual town behind the wall. Also, there was never a hole in the wall; the canyon wall had a slight notch through which the cattle could be run.

The Hole-In-The-Wall was a good hideout because the outlaws could see for miles in any direction from the top of the wall. Butch Cassidy supposedly said once that a dozen men could hold off a posse of 100 men from the walls of the Hole.[2] According to some researchers, Sundance visited the Hole shortly after his run-in with Deputy Sheriff James Swisher in Sundance, Wyo-

*Hole in the Wall area, Kaycee, Wyoming.
(Courtesy Sundance Properties.)*

ming.[3] In the Hole he likely would have met up with Elzy Lay and Flatnose George Currie, among others.

Today, the Hole is still a desolate, dry, ancient river bed, hidden by miles of steep, red desert wall. It is located on private property off Interstate 25. It can be visited by permission only but can be easily seen in the distance from the main road.

Next along the Outlaw Trail was Brown's Park, the most populated hideout.[4] It was in a valley 40 miles long and 6 miles wide, located along the Green River, and surrounded by Diamond and Cold Spring Mountains. Brown's Park was split between Utah and Colorado, with a very small section in Wyoming. The mountains protected the outlaws from severe winter weather; the river provided the valley with good grazing; and the

Entrance to John Jarvie's dugout.
(Courtesy Sundance Properties.)

state lines were invisible barriers against pursuing lawmen. The population of Brown's Park accepted the outlaws on the face of their local behavior. As long as a reputed outlaw earned his keep in the area peacefully, he was a welcome addition.

Today the area can be visited by following Colorado Route 318 West towards State Route 191 in Utah. Much of the road is a winding dirt trail, but it is well worth the day-long drive.

John Jarvie's homestead in Brown's Park is now preserved as a historical site by the Bureau of Land Management, which has purchased most of the land in the area. There is a two-room dugout on Jarvie's property in which Butch Cassidy, Sundance, and the gang often sought shelter.

A local story tells of the *Outlaws' Thanksgiving Dinner* around 1895.[5] Sundance, Butch and a few other outlaws played host to the community and prepared and

Another view of John Jarvie's hideout.
(Courtesy Sundance Properties.)

served a complete, traditional turkey dinner. The local families lent their finest linens, dishes, and silver for the evening, and they arrived dressed in their Sunday best.

Sundance greeted the guests at the hitching post of the Davenport Ranch on Willow Creek. After all of the guests arrived, he and Butch put on white butcher aprons and served their guests an elegant dinner. The party lasted into the wee hours of the morning with local entertainment and dancing. Ann Basset, who was at the dinner, later wrote her friend, Esther Campbell, that Sundance was tall, blond, and handsome, and that he had the young girls thoroughly enchanted the entire evening.

The last major hideout along the Outlaw Trail was Robbers Roost. It was located in the desert canyons of Utah, about midway between Moab and Hanksville. Not only was the Roost near the Utah and Colorado state line, but the numerous twisting canyons provided many hiding places for outlaws on the run. The area was inhospitable and very intimidating to those unfamiliar with the canyonlands. Therefore, few lawmen ever ventured after outlaws fleeing into the Roost area.

One who did, however, was Sheriff Tom Fares.[6] He followed Tom McCarty, Matt Warner, and Butch Cassidy into the Roost, and lost his way in the dry maze of canyons. Matt got the drop on him, gave him water, and headed him out of the Roost. However, Fares threatened to return to *get his man*, which made Matt and the others angry. They then took his saddle and pants and sent him riding towards Hanksville in just his underdrawers and riding bareback.

The Roost was probably the best-known to Sundance, as it was just over 100 miles from his cousin's home in Cortez, Colorado. Marvel Murdoch, the daughter of Elzy Lay, claimed that in the winter of 1896-1897 Sundance wintered at the Roost with his girlfriend, *Etta Place*, and Marvel's parents.[7]

Today the Roost is located on private property, reached by a very rough dirt road off Route 24. The surrounding area is in the Canyonlands National Park, in the high desert area where the Green River meets the Colorado River.

While not normally considered a major hideout on the Outlaw Trail, a ranch in New Mexico was also occasionally used by Sundance and the Wild Bunch. Butch Cassidy met Captain William French, part-owner of the WS Ranch in Alma. French did not know Butch's outlaw reputation; he only knew that he liked the work that Butch and his friends did when they were around the ranch. Therefore, whenever they showed up, French welcomed them.[8]

This safe haven was located near the Arizona state line and rather close to the border with Mexico as well. Although owned by another family now, the WS

Ranch is still a working ranch and still uses the WS name. Very little of the old town exists today, but it is easily reached on route 180, which goes directly past the ranch.

By 1897 to 1898 lawmen were finally beginning to tighten the noose around the neck of the Wild Bunch's doings. The ranchers thought it was not enough, and they often chided the law for not closing in on the gang's hideouts. However, to ride into one of these places was much easier said than done.

The Wild Bunch, The Outlaw Trail, and their hideouts have all become inseparable in Western history. Even today a ride through these areas has the flavor of a time gone by.

Notes

1. Horan, op cit, pages 227-233.
2. Patterson, op cit, page 205.
3. Garman, op cit, page 6.
4. William L. Tennent, *John Jarvie of Brown's Park*, Cultural Resources Series #7 of the Utah Bureau of Land Management, reprinted 1982; Diana Allen Kouris, *The Romantic and Notorious History of Brown's Park*, published 1988, Wolverine Gallery, Greybull, Wyoming, page 77.
5. Ibid, page 78; Tennent, op cit, pages 65-69; *The Denver Post*, November 20, 1977.
6. Warner, op cit, pages 136-143.
7. Baker, op cit, page 173; Betenson, op cit, page 121; Michael R. Kelsey, *Henry Mountains and Robbers Roost*, published 1987, Kelsey Publishing, Provo, Utah.
8. Captain William French, *Recollections of a Western Ranchman*, published reprint 1990, High-Lonesome Books, pages 251-283.

Harry A. Longabaugh.
(Courtesy The Pinkerton Detective Agency)

Chapter Eight

Ruthless But Loyal

It has been said, *The outlaws may have been tough, ruthless, even cruel to those they opposed - usually the rich and powerful - but they were true blue to their friends and families.*[1] That was probably an appropriate description of the personality of Sundance. He was a man of strong but often opposite characteristics.

Family members recalled that Sundance tried to stay in contact with his brothers and sisters. Pinkerton files recorded many of his visits and correspondence, especially with his brother, Elwood, and his sister, Samanna.[2] Sundance also kept in touch with his cousins in Cortez, Colorado, who were unknown to the law.[3] However, the family heartily disapproved of Sundance's activities as they were a conservative and religious family. Their disapproval was further verified by the dates of all known correspondence: their letters all occurred before his outlawry in the West and after he went *straight* in South America.[4]

One of Samanna's diary entries notes that she wrote to him on July 22, 1902; January 3, 1903; September 20, 1903; November 26, 1904; and April 22, 1905. Those dates all occurred while Sundance was ranching at Cholila in Argentina. Another sister, Emma, received a postcard from Sundance in 1904 from the St. Louis World's Fair, when he returned to the States for a visit.

A family friend living in Cortez shared her memory of Sundance.[5] When she was a very little girl, he came to visit her father and older brothers on business. The men were not home at the time, but they were expected to return soon. Sundance waited for them in her family's kitchen and visited with the remainder of the family. He was especially kind and friendly with the baby sister and reached down to pick her up. He bounced her on his knee, made a big fuss over her and created a very happy memory for an elderly woman today. According to family history, he had a tender spot for children, often remembering his nieces.

There were many recorded descriptions of Sundance by his fellow outlaws and by early Western researchers. Everyone seemed to most admire his quickness and accuracy with a gun.[6] He used a single shot Colt 45 almost exclusively. In *The Wild and Woolly, An Encyclopedia of the Old West*, Sundance was described as *the fastest gun in the Wild Bunch*.[7] Author Charles Kelly said Sundance was *pleasant, friendly, and cool in any emergency*.[8]

Walter Punteney, who participated in the Belle Fourche robbery with Sundance, once said that Sundance and Butch Cassidy ... *were not murderers. They would slip in some town and get the money and slip out again and they didn't want to hurt anybody*.[9] Punteney's nephew told me, *Uncle Walt was a good shot with a gun, but would never have wanted to have to face Sundance in a showdown. Sundance was an excellent gunsman*.[10]

Alan Swallow, in *The Wild Bunch*, described Sundance as *sullen and apt to drink too much*.[11] Harry Jr., on the other hand, claimed that his father only *drank moderately all through his adult life*.[12] He further stated that, *My old man was fast, but he would not push a man into a gun fight*. An acquaintance of Sundance's in South America once said, *He was as fast as a snake's tongue.*[13] In the *Bandit Invincible* manuscript, supposedly written by Butch Cassidy, Sundance is described quite well.[14] (The name "Maxwell" was used to disguise the identity of Sundance.)

> *Maxwell was a man about Butch's size and build but was slightly darker than Butch. He like Butch was quick as a steel trap in his movements and a dead shot.*

> *Maxwell was a natural born gentle man and had all the earmarks of one. Always emaculate (sic) in appearance and the attitude of the perfect gentle man. He like Cassidy was the champion of the under dog . . . Maxwell was not what one would call sullen, but he was Verry reserved and dispositioned to be distant except with his Verry closest friends and there were times when he held himself aloof from them. He was quick and active with a six shooter and if in a fit of temper or attacted he could shoot on the instant.*

Author J.D. Horan said Sundance *looked like a morose Swedish or German carpenter out of a job.*[15] This was rather appropriate as Sundance's family background was German, and his brother, Harvey, was a professional carpenter. Lula Parker Betensen, a sister of Butch Cassidy, wrote in her book, *He was a handsome man, quite tall and dark, and was a flashy dresser. An expert gunman, he had a quick, mean temper, and he was a killer.*[16] However, no proof was found to indicate that Sundance killed anyone. No wanted posters or warrants have been located that listed Sundance for murder.

In October, 1900, the Pinkertons received a description of Sundance from an informant, Charles Ayers, a Stock Association Inspector from Dixon, Wyoming.[17]

At the time of the report, Ayers apparently knew Sundance as *Harry Alonzo*. Sundance's use of the name "Alonzo" raises a question. Some researchers thought Sundance adopted the name from Alonzo Craven, the owner of the stolen gun and horse for which Sundance went to jail in Wyoming. Others say *Alonzo* is the middle name of Harry A. Longabaugh. Detractors point out that the name *Alonzo* sounds more Italian than German. However, Sundance's brother was named Harvey Sylvester Longabaugh, so *Alonzo* may well have been his middle name. Even the family does not know for certain, as only the initial *A* appears in any of the family records. Charles Ayers' description reads as follows:

> *32-5 ft 10. 175 - Med. Comp. firm expression in face, German descent Combs his hair Pompadour, it will not lay smooth - erect, but carries his head down not showing his eyes. eyes Blue or gray. Bowlegged - walks with feet far apart. Carries arms straight by his side. fingers closed, thumbs sticking straight out. eats Ralston food, asks for it, and discusses its merits he uses knife & fork awkwardly very quiet, cowboy. good Rider, marks his clothes "H L" with worsted thread - had catarrh badly*[18]

The Pinkerton's also described Sundance's habit of monogramming the initials H L on his clothing. Sundance's sister, Emma, was a dressmaker; maybe she taught her younger brother how to sew. Sewing in one form or another was a popular family ability. Sundance also had a cousin, Emma Ida Longabaugh, who had a millinery or hat-making business in Phoenixville, Pennsylvania.[19] Possibly Sundance was still wearing items marked with the HL brand of the N Bar N Ranch, Home Land and Cattle Company.

While there is no connection between the Ralston's for whom Sundance worked as a young boy and the cereal company, one wonders if his loyalty to an old employer had anything to do with his choice of Ralston cereals.[20]

Cattle Queen Ann Basset often spoke quite highly of Sundance and the kindnesses he showed to the residents of Brown's Park.[21] Acquaintances in South America also spoke well of him. Certainly Sundance and Butch Cassidy had a close and long-term friendship. Their loyalty to each other has never been questioned.

So, as an outlaw, Sundance was indeed tough and ruthless. To his family and friends, however, Harry A. Longabaugh was a kind and loyal human being. He just happened to rob banks for a living.

Notes

1. *Philadelphia Inquirer*, July 4, 1988.
2. Pinkerton, op cit.
3. Author's correspondence and interviews with descendants of George Longenbaugh.
4. Private family records.
5. Author's correspondence and interviews with descendants of George Longenbaugh.
6. Horan and Sann, op cit, page 96.
7. *The Wild and Woolly, An Encyclopedia of the Old West*, page copy supplied by Kerry Ross Boren, Manila, Utah.
8. Kelly, op cit, page 132.
9. Horan, op cit, page 246.
10. Author's correspondence with Al Punteney, California.
11. Alan Swallow, editor, *The Wild Bunch*, published 1966, Sage Books, Denver, Colorado, page 50.
12. Longabaugh Jr., lecture in Ogden, op cit.
13. Horan and Sann, op cit, page 96.
14. Pointer, op cit, pages 99-100.
15. Horan, op cit, page 240.
16. Betenson, op cit, page 115.
17. Pinkerton, op cit; Kouris op cit, page 98.
18. Pinkerton, op cit.
19. Private family records.
20. Author's correspondence and interviews with descendants of the Ralston family in Pennsylvania.
21. Tennent, op cit, page 65-69.

Part Two
(1890-1900)

November 29, 1892 — Malta train robbery

June 28, 1897 — Belle Fourche bank robbery

July 14, 1898 — Humboldt train robbery

April 3, 1899 — Elko saloon robbery

June 2, 1899 — Wilcox train robbery

September 19, 1900 — Winnemucca bank robbery

November 21, 1900 — Ft. Worth photo of the Wild Bunch

Chapter Nine

Malta

November 29, 1892

The mercury, which hovered about zero all day yesterday, went down to 16 degrees below last night. This morning the Missouri was frozen over, for the first time this season.[1]

The River Press of November 30, 1892 commented on the early cold snap. Many cowboys were laid off and were loitering around local bars, some looking for day work and others looking for mischief. As the winter weather set in and more hired hands were laid off, Sundance followed the road to Malta, Montana.

Sundance found an old friend, Bill Madden, from Mancos, Colorado. Together with another friend, Harry Bass, they hung out at Black's Saloon in Malta. The trio became especially friendly with saloon keeper Alex Black. (Another saloon keeper, C.W. Gardiner, later told the Pinkertons that Sundance had been in the Malta area for a while.)[2]

In 1892, Malta was not yet the county seat of Phillips County, as it was still part of Valley County.[3] In fact, it had only recently been named Malta and was previously called Siding 54. Malta was named for a British Island in the Mediterranean Sea and was so-named by a blindfolded railroad worker pointing on an old globe.[4] Its earliest history was as a trading post run by a buffalo bone merchant named Trafton.

The town grew quickly once the Great Northern Railroad came through the area.[5] Malta was in an area

Malta, Montana showing the railroad roundhouse and Malta Mercantile Company. (Courtesy Montana Historical Society.)

known as the cattle empire, with some of the largest cattle ranches of the day using the nearby open range. While the N Bar N Ranch was a good distance from Malta, it was within a full day's ride; and Sundance had ridden in off the range.

Sundance, Madden and Bass were amateurs, but a train robbery seemed just the thing to do for easy cash and a little excitement to ease the long, cold evenings. However, their inexperience eventually netted them more trouble than money.[6]

At 3 a.m. on Tuesday, November 29, 1892 the Great Northern westbound train #23 made its normal stop in Malta. Number 23 was an express train for passengers and mail from St. Paul, Minnesota to Butte, Montana. As the train pulled out, three masked men

Malta, Montana showing the Malta Mercantile Company. (Courtesy Montana Historical Society.)

jumped on the blind baggage car and told the engineer to stop the train near a fire about one mile ahead. When the train stopped, the engineer was told to have Mail Clerk Rawlins open the mail car.

Finding nothing there, two of the outlaws proceeded to the express car where Messenger Jerry Hauert was told to open the safes. The smaller safe contained a few packages of unknown value, $19.20 in cash, and two small pay checks. Check #27,482 was for R. White, and check #27,028 was for O.P. Bringham. Hauert did not have the combination for the large safe, so nothing else was stolen. One newspaper claimed that $25,000 was missed by the inept outlaws who believed Hauert, but it was common for only station agents to have this combination.

Malta, Montana railroad crossing, where the robbery took place today. (Courtesy Sundance Properties.)

Meanwhile the third outlaw was covering Conductor Bywater, the fireman, and the brakemen, who had all come to see what was happening with the engineer. The thieves were probably both frustrated and cold, but none of the passengers were bothered according to Conductor Bywater. In fact, the gang even offered the trainmen a drink before telling them to continue on their way.

Telegrams were soon wired in both directions along the track, and the express company offered a $500 reward for each of the thieves. The governor of Montana also offered a matching reward. One newspaper pointed out that the rewards were worth more than the outlaws had stolen, but it was important to capture the outlaws. The same paper also mentioned the obvious inexperience of these men since the express train had left St. Paul on a Sunday, not on a business day.[7]

Detective W. Black was hired by the Great Northern Railroad Company, and on December first he saw

Sheriff Hamilton of Cascade County, Sheriff B.F. O'Neal of Choteau County, Under-sheriff Matthews, and Harry Lund to enlist their help.[8] At 10 p.m. that night Harry Bass and Bill Madden (alias William Hunt) were arrested at Black's Saloon. At the same time, Alex Black (no relation to Detective Black) and Sundance were arrested as they boarded an eastbound train at the Malta train depot. Sundance was using two different names at the time of his arrest, J.E. Ebaugh and J.E. Thibadoe. The outlaws stay in Malta proved to be their downfall.

Detective Black had Conductor Bywater identify the outlaws and then took them to Helena, Montana to stand trial. Alex Black was released for lack of evidence; Harry Bass was given ten years, and Bill Madden was sentenced to fourteen years, both to be served in the penitentiary at Deer Lodge, Montana. Sundance escaped and was never brought to trial, but Bass and Madden both implicated him as being the third outlaw.[9]

Sundance headed across the open range he probably knew well from his N Bar N days, looking toward the Hole-In-The-Wall in Wyoming where friends and protection could be found.

Notes

1. *The River Press* (Malta), November 30, 1892.
2. Pinkerton, op cit.
3. Pamphlet, Phillips County Museum, Malta, Montana.
4. Ralph C. Henry, *Our Land Montana*, published 1969, State Publishing Company, page 378.
5. *Ibid*, pages 225-226.
6. All robbery details are taken from *The River Press* (Malta), November 30, 1892; *The Chinook Opinion*, December 1, 1892; *The Great Falls Daily Tribune*, November 30, 1892; *The River Press*, December 7, 1892; and *The Chinook Opinion*, December 8, 1892. All the newspaper articles were supplied by the Montana Historical Society, Helena, Montana.
7. *The Great Falls Daily Tribune*, November 30, 1892.
8. Kirby, op cit, page 95.
9. Pinkerton, op cit

$2500 REWARD

will be paid by us for the capture of the four men hereinafter described $625 reward will be paid for each man. These men are wanted for attempting to rob this bank on Monday June 28, 1897.

Description.

GEO. CURRIE--About 5 ft 10 in., weight 175, age 27, light complexion, high cheek bones, flat forehead, flat pug nose, big hands and bones, stoops a little, long light mustache, probably clean shaven.

HARVE RAY -- About 5 ft 8 1-2 in., weight 185, age 42, dark complexion, round full faced, bald headed, heavy long dirty brown mustache, might have heavy beard, dark gray eyes, hair quite gray above ears and inclined to curl, bow legged.

--**ROBERTS**--About 5 ft 7 1-2 in., age 39, rather small, weight about 140, very dark complexion, possibly quarter breed Indian. Formerly from Indian territory.

--**ROBERTS**--Rather small man. About 5 ft 6 in. weight 130, age 28, very dark, probably quarter breed Indian, large upper front teeth protruding from mouth.

$100 reward for information leading to their arrest. Please destroy former circulars.

BUTTE COUNTY BANK
Belle Fourche, S.D.

July 28, 1897

Text of a Pinkerton Wanted Poster.
(Courtesy Pinkerton Detective Agency.)

Chapter Ten

Belle Fourche

June 28, 1897

More accurate information is probably known about the Butte County Bank robbery in Belle Fourche, South Dakota, than any other robbery credited to Sundance. This is because some of the participants were caught and tried, and the court records are still in existence.

Belle Fourche, French for *beautiful fork*, was probably named for the meeting of the Belle Fourche and Redwater Rivers. The town is easily found today at the intersection of US 85 and US 212. Although the Butte County Bank building no longer stands, it was on the corner of what is today Sixth and State Streets.

Sundance undoubtedly knew Belle Fourche and the surrounding area quite well. He worked in the Black Hills area during the winter of 1886 to 1887.[1] The VVV (Three V) Ranch, where he had stolen the horse as a teenager, was only about 12 miles away. The town of Sundance, Wyoming, where he was jailed for 18 months, was less than 50 miles away.[2] Furthermore, it was quite possible that Sundance helped to plan this particular robbery in retribution against John Clay and Robert Robinson.[3] Clay and Robinson had been the manager and the trail boss of the VVV Ranch, and they were very much involved with Sundance's arrest and imprisonment in 1887. Ten years later, Clay and Robinson were the major stockholders of the Butte County Bank, also known as the Clay, Robinson and Company Bank. They

Belle Fourche Bank building.
(Courtesy Doug Engebretson.)

would be the ones most hurt by this holdup. Another manager of the VVV Ranch, James T. Craig, was the first person to suggest the outlaws were part of *the Curry gang from near Gillette.*[4]

The town of Belle Fourche nearly burned to the ground, including the jail, on September 25, 1895. A Civil War soldiers and sailors celebration was planned for the newly-built town on June 24 through the 26th, 1897. Sundance and his friends found this timing useful. There were many strangers in town for the celebration and an excess of money in the bank.

Sundance, Walt Punteney, Tom O'Day, Flatnose George Currie and Lonnie Logan made camp just east of town about Saturday, June 26th.[5] Using the celebration as cover, Tom O'Day went into Belle Fourche to case the town. He joined the revelers in Bruce Sabastian's Saloon before reporting back to the boys at camp.

Monday morning, June 28, 1897, O'Day again went into town alone, and the other four followed shortly behind him. According to Mr. W.F. Tracy's court testimony, O'Day went into Sabastian's Saloon about 9:30 that morning and purchased *two quart bottles of whiskey . . . and a pint bottle in his pocket.*[6] After getting on his horse and heading for Alanson Giles' Hardware Store, he returned to the saloon for another visit. The second visit was his mistake.

By 10 a.m. the rest of the gang had arrived in town and had hitched their horses near the side entrance of the bank. O'Day came out of the saloon and rode up to the front of the bank but did not tie his horse to the rail. By now the bank had been open for about an hour, and there were five customers in the lobby. The head cashier, Arthur H. Marble, and his assistant, S.W. Harry Ticknor, were behind the counter, and a local Methodist minister, Dr. E.E. Clough, was using a bank office.

Sundance and the others entered the front door and yelled, *Hold up your hands!* Cashier Marble reached for his pistol, but it misfired, and he too put up his hands. Meanwhile, from across State Street, in his hardware store, Mr. Giles looked through the bank windows and saw hands raised above heads. He ran out to investigate, but he was chased back into his own store by O'Day who was still outside the bank. O'Day's gunfire not only alerted the bank robbers inside but the local citizenry as well.[7]

Sundance quickly grabbed the $97 which Mr. Sam Arnold was depositing and escaped out the front door. In their hurry, the gang reportedly left over $1000 in gold and silver in a teller's tray behind the counter.[8] O'Day's horse was spooked by the gunfire and had run around the side of the bank. It began to follow the escaping outlaws down Sixth Street, over the railroad

Old Prison in Deadwood, South Dakota.
(Courtesy Deadwood Public Library.)

track, and up Sundance Hill, where it was shot by townsmen in pursuit.

O'Day attempted to escape on a nearby mule which proved to be too stubborn. He next tried to hide in an outhouse between Sabastian's Saloon and the printing office in the Andre Building. Mr. Rusaw Bowman stopped him as he came out, and held him at gunpoint while others searched his pockets. They found gun cartridges, $392.50 and a pint of whiskey, but no gun. They then turned over the outhouse and found the gun O'Day had hidden there. They promptly arrested the drunken O'Day and, ironically, confined him overnight in the bank vault because the Belle Fourche jail had again recently burned. The next day he was transferred to the Lawrence County jail in Deadwood, South Dakota.

Deadwood, South Dakota today from Mt. Moriah Cemetery. (Courtesy Sundance Properties.)

The other four outlaws headed southwest toward the VVV Ranch.[9] A reward of $100 was immediately posted for them and was later increased to $625 each.[10] A posse of nearly 100 men had them surrounded *in a small timber tract* but again they managed to escape.[11] The outlaws split up, and Flatnose and Logan headed for Baggs, Wyoming. It was said that the two Belle Fourche bank robbers shot up Jack Ryan's Bull Dog Saloon on July 29, 1897 and paid Ryan restitution of one silver dollar for each bullet hole.[12] Sundance took fifteen-year old Punteney along with him and headed for the Hole-In-The-Wall area.[13] There they remained hidden for a couple of months.

Sundance and Punteney soon met up with Harvey Logan, cousin to Lonnie Logan. They traveled north and arrived in Red Lodge, Montana on Saturday, September

Lavina, Montana after it was abandoned. Building at far right was a saloon. (Courtesy Montana Historical Society.)

18, 1897. It was possible they planned to hit the bank in Red Lodge. They tried to convince the town marshal, Byron St. Clair, to conveniently leave town for awhile. Instead, St. Clair reported them to Carbon County Sheriff John Dunn. *The Billings Gazette*, however, wrote that someone in Red Lodge recognized them and reported them to Sheriff Dunn.[14]

Either way, Dunn, Stock Detective J. Dick Hicks, and Attorney Oscar C. Stone followed them north to Columbus, where they were joined by Stock Detective W.D. Smith and Constable H.J. Calhoun.[15] From Columbus, they pursued the outlaws through Big Timber, past the John T. Murphy Ranch (where Sundance had once worked), and on to Widow Ranch near Painted Robe, where they added Billy Mendenhall to their posse.[16]

By Wednesday morning, September 22nd, the posse had arrived in Lavina, Montana.[17] Lavina was a small, sleepy town in the middle of nowhere 100 years ago. It is that today, and most of the town's approximately twenty original buildings still exist. Lavina is located on Route 3, about a half mile south of Route 12, and the Musselshell River runs past the edge of town.

Sundance, Logan and Punteney apparently did not know they were being followed because they stopped in Lavina to have a round of drinks at H.C. Jolly's saloon. They paid their bar bill with a $2.50 check from the Butte County Bank of Belle Fourche. *It is the supposition that this was one of the checks stolen from the robbed bank four months ago . . . these facts of themselves will be sufficient to convince most anybody that the men . . . are the ones who robbed the South Dakota bank.*[18] The Lavina stop brought the posse within forty-five minutes of the outlaws.

About twenty miles north of Lavina, Sundance and the others started to set up camp for the night at a spring on the Musselshell River. Logan was picketing his horse, and Sundance and Punteney were going to the spring for water when the posse suddenly appeared less than 100 yards away.

Punteney immediately jumped behind the edge of a small bluff hiding the spring and took aim with his Winchester. Sundance pulled a trick from his younger days, when he had hoped to become a horse rider in a rodeo. *He made a rush for his horse and spring [sic] into the saddle. He then drew his Winchester and, Indian fashion, slid down on the opposite side of the horse from the posse.*[19] However, the startled horse bolted across the spring, fell and broke its neck. Sundance jumped free of the falling horse and joined Punteney behind the edge of the bluff.

Meanwhile, Logan had reached his horse and began racing towards the nearby field of buffalo grass. The posse fired shots after the fleeing outlaw, hitting the horse three times. The horse continued running for about a mile before it dropped dead, throwing Logan clear. One of the bullets had passed through the horse and had hit Logan in the wrist, causing an injury which was used to identify him for the remainder of his life. The posse caught up with him as he hid in a buffalo grass wallow, and he surrendered.[20]

Sundance and Punteney had not been able to shoot their way to freedom either. Although little gun play had actually taken place, the posse noted that *a regular arsenal of arms* was captured in the outlaws' possession.[21] They also took seven horses and the saddles and bedrolls from the two dead horses.

The three outlaws were taken by stagecoach to Billings and held as fugitives from justice in the Belle Fourche robbery. By Saturday, September 25th, S.W. Ticknor had arrived from Belle Fourche to identify the trio, which he did on Sunday morning. On Monday, September 27th, they were taken before Alex Fraser, Justice of the Peace, and again identified by Ticknor.

They claimed innocence and used the names Frank and Thomas Jones and Charley Frost. They hired lawyer J.B. Herford to defend them and paid him with their extra horses and gear.[22] After he heard Ticknor's testimony, Herford advised Sundance and the others to waive the governor's requisition, a legal formality, and return to South Dakota. The posse members put in a claim for the $1875 reward, $625 for each outlaw, at this same time.

Tuesday, September 28th, Detective Hicks and Smith of the Montana Stock Growers Association escorted Sundance, Logan and Punteney on the noon Burlington train to Deadwood, where they were placed

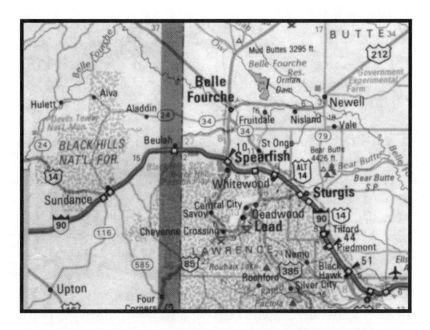

Area map around Deadwood, South Dakota.

in the Lawrence County jail.[23] Mr. Marble and Mr. Ticknor of the Belle Fourche bank each identified the men as the bank robbers at the preliminary hearing on Thursday, September 30, 1897. The grand jury indicted the men and placed bail at $10,000 each.

At the time of his arraignment in Deadwood, Sundance again gave his name as Frank Jones, his well-used alias from Montana days. He, Logan and Punteney were placed in jail with Tom O'Day, who had been previously captured. Their jail was an old building with dugout cells on the corner of what today is Washington and Monroe Streets in Deadwood's residential section.

On October 13, 1897, Frank Jones filed an affidavit on behalf of himself and his co-defendants proclaiming their innocence and asking for more time to prove their case. While awaiting their court appearance, the prisoners were apparently allowed occasional freedom in an area known as the *Bull Pen*, possibly an exercise yard.[24] This provided an opportunity for escape when a friend on the outside left four provisioned horses near the jail. According to a deposition found in Sheriff Frank Hadsell's papers, the horses may have been supplied by Logan's cousin, Lonnie.[25]

On Sunday, October 31, 1897 about 9 p.m., Deputy Sheriff John Marshall and his wife arrived to lock the prisoners in their cells for the night. He was immediately knocked down, and he and his wife were then locked in the jail. All four of the Belle Fourche prisoners and William Moore, a fellow prisoner, escaped quickly and easily. Within an hour of the jailbreak, over sixty men from the nearby towns had become a posse in pursuit.

Tom O'Day and Walt Punteney were recaptured near Spearfish, South Dakota, and again held for trial. O'Day was later found innocent, and Punteney was released without trial due to lack of evidence. All trace of Moore, the other prisoner, was lost after he stole two horses from a former employer.[26] (Author F. Bruce Lamb claims that the outlaw known in later years as Speck was the mulatto who escaped from Deadwood with Sundance and Logan.[27]) Sundance and Logan made a clean escape and headed for Montana. Sheriff Butts of Butte County and the VVV Ranch Manager J.T. Craig followed closely but never caught them.

The American Bankers Association and the Union Pacific Railroad hired the Pinkerton National Detective Agency just about this time. It was hoped that their presence would stop the outlaws, if not capture them.

According to researchers Pearl Baker and Ed Kirby, Sundance then wintered either in southeastern Arizona or on the W S Ranch in Alma, New Mexico.[28] Both agree that by the spring of 1898 Sundance was in Nevada, traveling by train from Green River, Utah.

Notes

1. *Daily Yellowstone Journal*, June 9, 1887.
2. Crook County, Wyoming, Court Records, as supplied by Mary Garman.
3. *The Pioneer Times* (Black Hills), June 29, 1897.
4. *The Sundance Gazette*, July 2, 1897.
5. All robbery court testimony and records were provided by Doug Engebretson of Belle Fourche, South Dakota.
6. Doug Engebretson, *Empty Saddles, Forgotten Names,* published 1984, North Plains Press, Aberdeen, South Dakota, pages 171-181.
7. *Ibid.*
8. *The Billings Gazette*, September 28, 1897.
9. *The Pioneer Times*, June 29, 1897.
10. *The Sundance Gazette*, July 2, 1897.
11. *Ibid.*
12. Patterson, op cit, page 201; Kelly, op cit, page 160; Pointer, op cit, page 130.
13. *The Billings Gazette*, September 24, 1897.
14. *The Billings Times*, September 30, 1897.
15. *The Billings Gazette*, September 24 and 28, 1897.
16. *Freemont County Clipper*, October 1897.
17. *The Billings Times*, September 30, 1897.
18. *The Billings Gazette*, September 24, 1897.
19. *Ibid.*
20. *The Billings Times*, September 30, 1897.
21. *The Billings Gazette*, September 24, 1897.
22. *The Billings Times*, September 30, 1897.
23. *Sturgis Weekly Record,* October 1, 1897; *Queen City Mail of Belle Fourche*, September 29, 1897.
24. Court Records; Kirby, op cit, page 62.
25. Sheriff Frank Hadsell, private papers H70-18/107-125, Wyoming State Archives, Cheyenne, Wyoming.
26. Court Records.
27. Lamb, op cit, page 153.
28. Kirby, op cit, page 63; Baker, op cit, page 100.

*Charles Siringo, on the left, was one of
the most famous of the Pinkerton agents.
The man on his right is Pawnee Bill.*

Chapter Eleven

The Pinkertons

Allan Pinkerton was born on August 25, 1819 in Glasgow, Scotland. He might well be described as a liberal revolutionary today. He was an agitator for workers' rights in Scotland, and he immigrated to the United States in 1842 in order to escape arrest. He immediately picked up the abolitionists cause and aided many runaway slaves in reaching the Canadian borders.[1]

In 1850 Pinkerton opened the North Western Police Agency in Chicago, Illinois. He worked closely with the railroads capturing holdup men and organizing a guard force on board the trains.

It was at this time that he met a young railroad lawyer named Abraham Lincoln. In February 1861, Pinkerton's railroad undercover work resulted in his discovery of a plot to assassinate the then President-elect Lincoln. After he took office, Lincoln asked Pinkerton (using the alias of Major E.J. Allen) to set up a Union spy system. In later years, this same system became the Federal Secret Service, which in turn served as a primary concept for the Federal Bureau of Investigation or the FBI.

After the Civil War, Pinkerton re-named his agency Pinkerton's National Detective Agency and used

97

an open eye as his logo. This was the creation of *the private eye.* Pinkerton took fierce pride in his work and accomplishments and once wrote, *I do not know the meaning of the word 'fail.' Nothing in hell or heaven can influence me when I know that I am right.*

Pinkerton was not completely successful in his attempt to rid the railroads of outlaw gangs. The James Gang, the Wild Bunch and other groups of outlaws continued to prey upon banks and trains with relative ease.

Allan Pinkerton's death in 1884 did not end the Agency. His sons William and Robert took over with even more enthusiasm to thwart these outlaws. They may have begun to use somewhat unethical methods of detecting. In a letter written by William A. Pinkerton in 1921, he said, *We did have to do with the breaking up of the 'Wild Bunch' and the killing off of a number of them.* A letter written in 1910 stated, *We hope someday to apprehend these people in this country or through our correspondents get them killed in the Argentine Republic.*[2] Their constant frustration in tracking down Sundance, Butch and the others seemed to make the Pinkertons even more desperate to catch them. They wanted the outlaws at any cost.

Most of the expense in tracking Sundance and the others was paid for by the American Bankers Association after the Winnemucca, Nevada bank robbery. However, *The Pinkerton Agency, through its personal interest in these parties, and on one occasion at the agency's expense sent an official from the New York Office to the Argentine Republic to endeavor to get information and locate the remaining members of this band.*[3] This was undoubtedly when agent Frank P. Dimaio was assigned to the case in South America. A letter written to a Major Richard Sylvester said, *The American Bankers Association would permit us to follow this case up, but they would not permit the expense. And therefore we have been keeping a run on these people in our own way.*[4]

Eventually, Allan Pinkerton's grandsons inherited the Agency, and all of the Wild Bunch members were presumed dead or in jail. The last known mention of Sundance in the Pinkerton files appeared in a letter dated 1921 which stated, *the last we heard of Longbaugh . . . he was in jail in Peru . .* In April, 1930, Chapman's article about the Bolivian shootout appeared in the *Elks Magazine*, and the Pinkerton's wholeheartedly agreed, closing the books forever.

In 1987, the Pinkerton's Detective Agency was purchased by California Plant Protection, a security and investigation firm in California. The newly combined companies, CPP/Pinkerton, employ over 55,000 nationwide today.

Notes

1. Information compiled from *Encyclopedia Brittanica,* 1960 edition, "Allan Pinkerton;" *Funk & Wagnalls New Encyclopedia,* 1973 edition, "Allan Pinkerton;" *Los Angeles Times,* February 20, 1989.
2. Pinkerton Files, memo dated November 17, 1921 signed Wm. A. Pinkerton; unsigned letter to Major Richard Sylvester from the Pinkerton office, dated March 5, 1910.
3. Pinkerton Files, op cit.
4. *Ibid.*

Chapter Twelve

Humboldt

July 14, 1898

When Louis Barbeau discovered silver in the canyons of Comstock, Nevada, the rush began.[1] In 1860 the Humboldt Mining District was established, and the city of Humboldt grew overnight.[2] In 1863, the successful mining city boasted of its *200 houses, two hotels, two saloons, blacksmith shop*, and a population of 500.[3]

However, in 1865 there was a silver panic in the financial world, nearby miners were striking, and the comfortable world of Humboldt City began to crumble. By 1869 the city was all but deserted, with only a few townspeople electing to remain.[4]

One of the few business still in town was the once-elegant Humboldt House, a combination hotel, restaurant and railroad depot. In its prime, the depot was a beautiful stopover, with its outside fountain and surrounding gardens and shade trees. Travelers could enjoy *the best meal on the line; cost 75 cents in coin or $1 in paper.*[5]

Today all that remains of Humboldt are a few ruins nestled up against the canyon walls and the 125-year old trees which once surrounded the Humboldt House at the railroad crossing. The depot is gone and a small house now sits in the shade once enjoyed by travelers along the Southern Pacific train lines. It can be reached 4.5 miles southeast of Interstate 80, about 35 miles west of Winnemucca, Nevada.

By the summer of 1898, Sundance, Harvey Logan (Kid Curry) and Flatnose George Currie were in the area of what was then called Humboldt County.[6] Sundance may have originally headed northwest to look up his cousin, Seth Longabaugh. Seth was a mason in the mining town of Eureka, Nevada, about 150 miles southeast of Humboldt.[7] He moved west from Pennsylvania and was a barkeeper, and Sundance visited him quite often over the next two years or more.

On July 14, 1898 the Southern Pacific passenger train #1, traveling east, arrived on time at the Humboldt House Station.[8] As the train pulled out of the depot at 1:25 a.m., two outlaws boarded the rear of the tender. A mile up the track, they climbed over the tender and covered the engineer and the fireman with their revolvers. The train was stopped immediately, but the thieves ordered the engineer to pull about a mile further up the track to a large pile of railroad ties, where a third outlaw was apparently waiting with the horses. He was thought to be a Negro, but he was only dark-skinned and tanned.

Unknown to the outlaws, the rear brakeman had realized the situation and had jumped off the train and headed back to Humboldt. From there he telegraphed Winnemucca, which was the next large stop. A special train car and posse began to ready.

Meanwhile, the express messenger was ordered to open the express car door. When he refused, a stick of dynamite was exploded at the rear door in warning. The engineer and fireman then suggested that the agent come out before he was blown up along with the train. They also asked him not to come out shooting, fearful that they would be caught in the crossfire. So, he opened the express car door.

The railroad station at Humboldt House. (Courtesy Nevada Historical Society.)

While one thief covered the engineer, fireman and messenger at a distance, the second outlaw set more dynamite, ripping open the train roof as well as the safe. They took about $450 in cash and some jewelry, and wrapped their feet in empty money sacks to disguise their bootprints.[9]

Telling the engineer to board the train and pull out, they then disappeared around the pile of railroad ties, jumped on their horses and escaped.[10] The train and express companies immediately posted a $1000 reward for the outlaws. The special train car from Winnemucca met the Southern Pacific #1 at Mill City, about ten miles east of the holdup site and quickly dispatched the posse on the robbers' trail. However, the outlaws had split up as usual and thereby escaped.

In April of the following year, two men named Shaw and Bowie were tried in Winnemucca for the Humboldt train robbery.[11] Although J.N. Thacker, a detective for Wells, Fargo & Company felt they were guilty, one of the jury members provided the defendants

The ruins of the Humboldt railroad station hidden behind the trees. (Courtesy Sundance Properties.)

with an alibi, claiming to have seen them in Lovelock on the day of the robbery. Thus, they were acquitted. Sundance, Logan and Flatnose had again escaped justice.

Notes

1. Dave Basso, *Ghosts of Humboldt Region*, published 1970, Western Printing & Publishing Company, page 35.
2. Stanley W. Paher, *Nevada Ghost Towns & Mining Camps*, published 1970, Howell-North Books, page 132.
3. Basso, op cit, page 35.
4. *Ibid.*
5. Paher, op cit, page 131-132.
6. Baker, op cit, pages 100-101; Kirby, op cit, pages 65-66.
7. Pinkerton Files; Thompson and West, *History of Nevada 1881*, published 1958, Howell-North, Berkeley, California, pages 237-239; U.S. Census Records.
8. *The Weekly Independent* (Elko), July 15, 1898.
9. *Ibid*, July 22, 1898.
10. *Ibid*, July 15, 1898.
11. *The Free Press* (Elko), April 29, 1899.

Chapter Thirteen

Elko

April 3, 1899

Elko, Nevada was a town in which one could easily hide. It grew from a tent city in the 1860's named for the many elk in the area. It was located at the end of the railroad line, where passengers boarded stagecoach lines to finish their journey. By 1899 Elko's local newspaper wrote, *For some time past Elko has been harboring many tough characters.*[1] Today, Elko is a populated county seat about 300 miles east of Reno, Nevada and 200 miles west of Salt Lake City, Utah on Interstate 80.

Sundance, Harvey Logan and Flatnose George Currie stayed in Elko at Johnny Craig's place for about a week.[2] They were using the names Frank Bozeman, Joe Stewart and John Hunter, and they had quickly earned a reputation as big spenders. *They displayed considerable money while there, several times breaking hundred dollar bills.*[3]

Railroad Street is now Elko's main street. In 1899, it had a number of saloons. One of the saloons was the Club Saloon, owned by Mr. E.M. James Gutridge. The Club Saloon frequently advertised in the local paper, and continued in business until September 30, 1918.[4] The outlaws' original plan to hold up the local

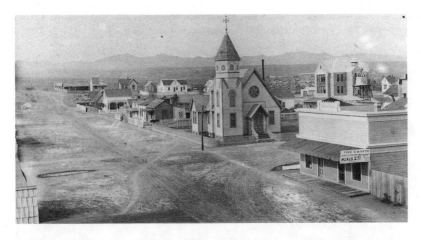

Elko, Nevada circa 1896. (Courtesy Northeastern Nevada Museum.)

bank was modified when the saloon was rumored to have a large amount of cash in their safe.

On Monday night, April 3, 1899, Gutridge closed up at midnight. Elko's Constable, Joe Triplett, had just left, and C.B. Nichols, the night bartender, was the only other person in the saloon. As Gutridge and Nichols were counting the evening receipts at the open safe behind the bar, three masked men came in with drawn revolvers.[5]

Gutridge unsuccessfully hollered for Triplett and was hit on the side of the head for his attempt. While one outlaw covered the door, another one took Gutridge and Nichols around to chairs in front of the bar. The third outlaw then cleaned out the safe, said to have been only $550. However, later rumors put the take at $3000.[6]

Sundance, Logan, and Currie warned Gutridge to stay seated and quiet for two minutes while they backed out of the saloon towards their horses. By the time the alarm had been given, the outlaws had escaped towards Tuscarora, Nevada.[7]

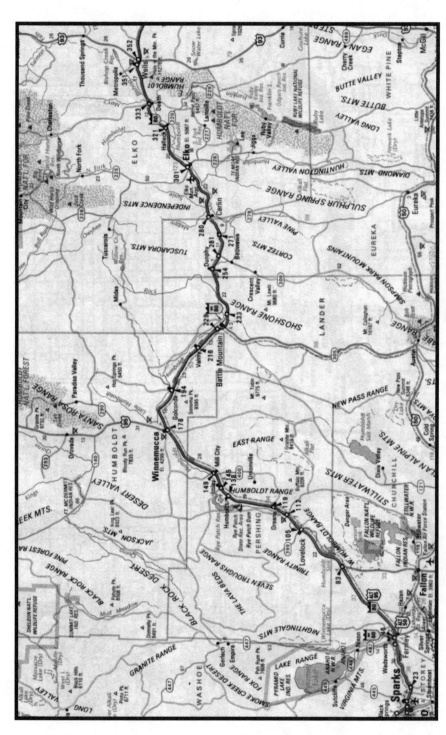

Area map of the Wild Bunch robberies that occured in Nevada

Gutridge immediately suspected three locals named John Page, J. Cook, and Bart Holbrook. However, when they were brought before Justice Morgan, they had sound alibis and were consequently freed. Gutridge then suspected Bozeman, Stewart, and Hunter. All three had left town the same night.

When the bank of Winnemucca, Nevada was held up a year and a half later, Johnnie Vargas recognized the bank thieves. They were the same men he had known in Elko, only 125 miles away, as Bozeman, Stewart, and Hunter.[8] Furthermore, Vargas pointed out, the outlaws were again escaping in the direction of Tuscarora, where the trio had last been seen.

Notes

1. *The Elko Free Press*, April 8, 1899.
2. *Ibid.*
3. *The Free Press* (Elko), September 29, 1900.
4. *Ibid.*
5. *The Elko Free Press*, April 8, 1899.
6. Kirby, op cit, page 66; Baker, op cit, page 101.
7. *The Elko Free Press*, April 8, 1899.
8. *The Free Press* (Elko), September 29, 1900.

Wilcox Train Robbery, Union Pacific wreck, June 2, 1899, view of safe which was blown open. (Courtesy Wyoming State Archives.)

Chapter Fourteen

Wilcox

June 2, 1899

Wilcox, Wyoming, was a very small railroad town on the Union Pacific Railroad, 14 miles southeast of Medicine Bow and 4 miles northwest of Rock River, Wyoming. Today, the town no longer exists but is still a switching station beside the railroad tracks which run past the old townsite. It can be reached off Route 287 and is clearly visible from the road.

At 2:18 a.m. on Friday, June 2, 1899, the Union Pacific Overland Flyer #1 was flagged down by an emergency flare at milepost #609.[1] Thinking that a nearby bridge might be out, the engineer, W.R. Jones, stopped the train. Two outlaws quickly lit dynamite fuses on the bridge, boarded the train, and ordered Jones and the fireman, Mr. Dietrick, to move across the bridge. When Jones reacted too slowly, one of the outlaws hit him in the head with his six-shooter.

The train was across the bridge before it blew up. The tourist cars were uncoupled from the engine, baggage, mail, and express cars. Jones was then ordered to pull another two miles up the track towards Medicine Bow where four more outlaws were waiting. Meanwhile, the conductor, Mr. Storey, was warning those on the second section not to interfere.[2]

Remains of Express car dynamited in Wilcox Robbery on Union Pacific Railroad, June 1899. (Courtesy Wyoming State Archives.)

Three of the robbers, accompanied by Trainmen Jones and Dietrick, then ordered the mail clerks, Robert Lawson and Burt Bruce, to open up the mail car doors. Bruce refused, and the robbers blew open the doors. They then ordered express car messenger Charles E. Woodcock to open the express car door. He refused also, and they again turned to dynamite to open the door. This explosion slightly injured Woodcock, and he had to be helped from the train.

More dynamite was used to blow open the express car safes. The charge must have been too strong, because the express car was blown to pieces by the force. (One newspaper account said the outlaws used a total of 200 pounds of dynamite, all stolen from a nearby railroad

*Wilcox Train Robbery, June 2, 1899. Baggage Car,
shows safe taken in railroad yard, Laramie, Wyoming.
(Courtesy Wyoming State Archives.)*

work crew.)[3] Sundance and the gang picked up between
thirty and sixty thousand dollars, some of it in unsigned
bank notes, and a number of diamonds. (Part of the
discrepancy about the amount taken was because some
was later recovered.) Their work had taken them nearly
two hours, but they escaped in a northerly direction,
towards Hole-In-The-Wall.

As usual the gang split up and it began to rain
quite hard.[4] These two factors helped slow the posses as
they followed the outlaws. Flatnose George Currie led
half of the outlaws to the area of the Hole-In-The-Wall
in a clean escape. Meanwhile, the other three outlaws
rode south and were followed for a short distance by a
posse led by Sheriff Swanson out of Rock Springs.[5]

111

A list of stolen items included four Elgin watches, 19 scarf pins and 29 gold-plated cuff button pairs. The Pacific Express Company also listed the serial numbers of the unsigned banknotes which had been stolen. The total cash amounted to $3400, most of which had torn corners as a result of the robbery. (Those torn portions would later help to identify the money.)[6]

Finley P. Grindley, a passenger, scouted the area and soon found a fifty-pound sack of dynamite, hobbled relay horses, and supplies. They were all within a mile of the tracks.[7] He also was said to have seen Mr. Preston A. Douglas, a lawyer friend of Butch Cassidy, at the scene. A short while later, the train was underway towards Medicine Bow. Posses were immediately raised, and telegrams were wired to the railhead and to Sheriff McDaniel of Rawlins, Wyoming. By 9:00 a.m. a specially outfitted railroad car posse had arrived at Medicine Bow and within twenty-four hours there were nearly 100 men out in posses. Posses also left from Laramie, Casper, and Lander in an attempt to surround and cut off the escaping thieves.[8] One of the posses even brought bloodhounds, but to no avail.[9]

A posse of 14 men, with Sheriff Josiah (Joe) Hazen of Converse County in charge, caught up with the gang near Horse Ranch, Wyoming.[10] Al Hudspeth, of the C Y Ranch, noticed them in a cabin near his range and reported their presence to the Casper authorities. This put the posse back on their trail. When the posses closed in on the outlaws, they started a gunfight and Sheriff Hazen was fatally wounded.[11] (*The Carbon County Journal* later reported a collection for Hazen's family had reached $10,000.)[12] Reports said that the outlaws were equipped with smokeless powder which had just been introduced.

After the ambush, the posse members remained under cover. This allowed the outlaws, who were on foot, to escape. When they abandoned their horses, they also abandoned some of their plunder.[13] In a search through Sheriff Frank Hadsell's private correspondence, a diary entry reads, *(Charles) Woodward says White River Charlie, Jack McKnight, and Hank Boyed alias Longbaugh killed Hazen.*[14] A member of the posse named Buck said that all six outlaws were at the scene of the ambush.[15]

The outlaws most often credited with this robbery are Sundance, Harvey Logan (Kid Curry), Flatnose George Currie, Lonnie Logan, Bill Carver, and Ben Kilpatrick (The Tall Texan). Others listed as possible participants included Bill Cruzan, O.E. Hanks, Bill Jones, and Elzy Lay. Butch Cassidy was often listed as the mastermind, in spite of his promise to Governor DeForest Richards of Wyoming. (In order to gain parole, Butch had promised to stay out of the state of Wyoming when perpetrating any crimes.) This theory gained weight from the fact that the posses found an extra set of tracks joining the thieves the next day.[16] While there were only six outlaws present during the actual robbery, the others may have been involved in the planning stages or with the escape relays. One newspaper article alluded to the outlaws' many powerful friends who apparently helped them during their escape.[17]

By June 10, 1899, the Union Pacific and the Pacific Express Railroads had jointly issued a wanted poster for the six bandits.[18] They offered $2000 per head, dead or alive. The U.S. Government further offered $1000 per outlaw. This brought the total reward for the entire gang to $18,000.

Two weeks after the robbery, the famous Pinkerton detective Charles A. Siringo began following the gang members who were riding south. Siringo suspected one of them to be Harvey Logan (Kid Curry). The trail led over the Colorado River and through the Carlisle Ranch near Monticello, Utah. The outlaws were said to be riding hard, towards the south, with Siringo only a week behind them. He trailed them through Cortez, Mancos, and Durango, Colorado, where some unsigned bank notes from the Wilcox robbery had been passed.[19] After following a number of false leads, Siringo was three weeks behind and finally lost the trail on the Mississippi River. Bank notes had also been passed in Alma, New Mexico, one of Butch's old strongholds, and in Harlem, Montana, in The Curry Brother's saloon owned by Lonnie Logan.[20] The gang had obviously dispersed into a large area.

Sundance was one of the other outlaws with Logan. He was returning "home" to safety. He knew the area around Durango and Cortez well since he had lived there with his cousins. He was sure to receive the protection and the provisions which he needed while planning his next move. George Longenbaugh's wife, Mary, often took him perishables such as butter and eggs when he was hiding nearby. Kid Curry continued on to the Sand Gulch Ranch.[21]

Later, in four consecutive issues of the Rawlins weekly newspaper *Carbon County Journal*, the capture of two men suspected of being the Wilcox outlaws was reported.[22] Postal Clerk Dietrick was sent to Dillon, Montana, to identify them, but he could not. Because the thieves had worn white masks, Dietrick was uncertain. Follow-up stories identified the men as Dave Putty and Bud Nolan and then later accounts acknowledged that they were not the Wilcox outlaws known as the Roberts Brothers. Sundance had escaped again.

Notes

1. *Carbon County Journal,* June 3, 1899; Horan, op cit, page 251; Baker, op cit, pages 101-102.
2. *The Buffalo Bulletin,* June 8, 1899; Carbon County Journal, June 3, 1899.
3. *Ibid.*
4. Kelly, op cit, page 242; Alfred James Mokler, *The History of Natrona County,* Wyoming, 1888-1922, published 1923, R.R. Donnelley & Sons Company, Chicago, page 320.
5. Charles A. Siringo, *A Cowboy Detective,* published 1988, University of Nebraska Press, pages 312-324.
6. Sheriff Frank Hadsell's private papers H70-18/98, Wyoming State Archives, Cheyenne, Wyoming.
7. *The Buffalo Bulletin,* June 8, 1899.
8. *Carbon County Journal,* June 3, 1899.
9. *Ibid,* June 24, 1899.
10. *Natrona County Tribune,* June 8, 1899; Carbon County Journal, June 17, 1899.
11. *Ibid,* June 10, 1899.
12. *Ibid,* June 17, 1899.
13. *Ibid,* June 10, 1899; Mokler, op cit, page 318.
14. Sheriff Frank Hadsell's private papers and correspondence, #H83-62/ 28, in the Wyoming State Archives, Cheyenne, Wyoming.
15. *Carbon County Journal,* June 10, 1899.
16. John Cornelison, *The Wilcox Train Robbery,* Historical Research Department, Wyoming State Archives, page 4.
17. *Carbon County Journal,* June 24, 1899.
18. Horan, op cit, page 252; Siringo, op cit, pages 324, 336, 340 and 367.
19. Kelly, op cit, page 248; Pointer, op cit, page 156.
20. *Ibid,* Siringo, op cit, pages 324, 336, 340 and 367; Brekke, op cit, page 52.
21. Author's correspondence and interview with descendants of George Longenbaugh; Lamb, op cit, page 3. McCarty, op cit, pages 1, 26-28 and 54; Churchill, op cit, page 16.
22. *Carbon County Journal,* July 3-24, 1899; Pence and Hunter, op cit, page 100.

$4000 REWARD

By Union Pacific Railroad Company.

Second Section Train No. 3 Held Up by Four Masked Men,

ABOUT TWO AND ONE HALF MILES WEST OF TIPTON, SWEETWATER CO., WYO., AT 8:30 P. M. AUGUST 29, 1900.

$8,000.00 REWARD!

In ADDITION to the reward of $1,000 EACH offered by the Union Pacific Railroad Company for the capture of the men, dead or alive, who robbed Union Pacific train No 3, near Tipton, Wyo., on the evening of August 29th, 1900, the Pacific Express Company, on the same conditions, hereby also offers a reward of $1,000.00 for each robber.

THE PACIFIC EXPRESS COMPANY.

August 31st, 1900.

Green River, Wyo., September 1st, 1900.

Dear Sir:-

Our money loss is $50.40, damage to car safe and express freight will amount to $3000.00. Robbers used Kepauno Chemical Co., Giant Powder, dated September 15th, 1899. Ashburn Mo. Works, forty percent.

Yours truly,

(signed) F. C. Gentsch, Gen'l Supt.

Reward Poster. (Courtesy Union Pacific Railroad.)

Chapter Fifteen

Tipton
August 29, 1900

Tipton was a small rail town with its only population the families of railroad workers who lived there to refuel or load water for passing trains. The buildings were razed recently, but the townsite is located just over a rise on a short dirt road which turns south from Interstate 80.

Pinkerton interviews after the robbery indicated that at least some of the gang were in the area and checked out the situation prior to the actual robbery.[1] The Pinkerton report listed a Mr. and Mrs. William Running as operating a *company eating house* in Tipton. The Runnings said that they recognized some of the gang. A waitress, Lizzie Warren, said she had served one of the robbers a meal. Mr. A. Iverson of nearby Red Desert saw two of the men a *couple of days before the robbery*. Mr. Joe J. Maloney, a visitor to the area, said he also saw two of the gang two or three days before and could identify one.

The outlaws must have been satisfied with what they saw. On Wednesday, August 29, 1900, about 2:30 a.m., the Union Pacific passenger train No. 3 made its scheduled stop at Tipton, Wyoming.[2] The train took on water and continued heading west towards Table Rock. Mr. and Mrs. Running claimed they saw a man heading

117

*Union Pacific posse of the best trackers and marksmen
in the West. (Courtesy Union Pacific Railroad.)*

for the engine as well as at least one more man nearby.
The tracks led upgrade a mile or two out of town, so the
train was moving slowly. A fire signal was spotted,
waving them to stop next to milepost #740.4.[3]

Engineer Henry Wollenstein stopped the train,
and the gang ordered Conductor E.J. Kerrigan to un-
hitch the engine, baggage, and express cars.[4] Mr.
Kerrigan insisted on setting the brakes for the first
section of cars and then warned the passengers to keep
their heads inside the train windows. The detached cars
were then moved a short distance away while the robbers held their Winchesters on the crewmen. When the
train stopped again, the outlaws ordered the train messenger to open up the express car. Ironically, it was
Charles E. Woodcock, the same messenger who was
injured in the blast at the Wilcox Siding robbery. Woodcock again refused to open the doors until Mr. Kerrigan
convinced him that dynamite was being readied to blow
the doors open anyway. During all that time, Woodcock
hid two packages of money from the safe behind a nearby
trunk.[5]

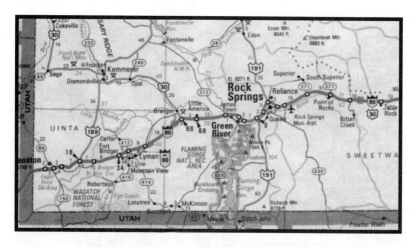

Map of area near Tipton, Wyoming.

According to the *Daily Pottstown Ledger* of August 31, 1900, it took three charges to blow open the safe.[6] In the process, the robbers also managed to blow the roof, sides, and ends out of the baggage car and the car next to it. (Since the *Daily Pottstown Ledger* was the largest newspaper in the area where Sundance's Pennsylvania family lived, you can imagine their curiosity and concern when they read this detailed report, headlined *Another Train Robbery*.) The article further stated that *it took the gang about an hour to complete their work*. They did not rob any passengers or trainmen, stating that they meant no personal harm to any of those people.

The outlaws gathered up the money and made their escape in a southeasterly direction. The train continued on to Green River.[7] When the train arrived, it was two hours late, and an alarm was quickly raised. With rewards of $1000 for each outlaw offered, at least three posses went out after them.[8] The posse leaders were Timothy T. Keliher of the Union Pacific Mounted

Express car blown up in holdup by Wild Bunch (Courtesy Union Pacific Railroad, H-15-6.)

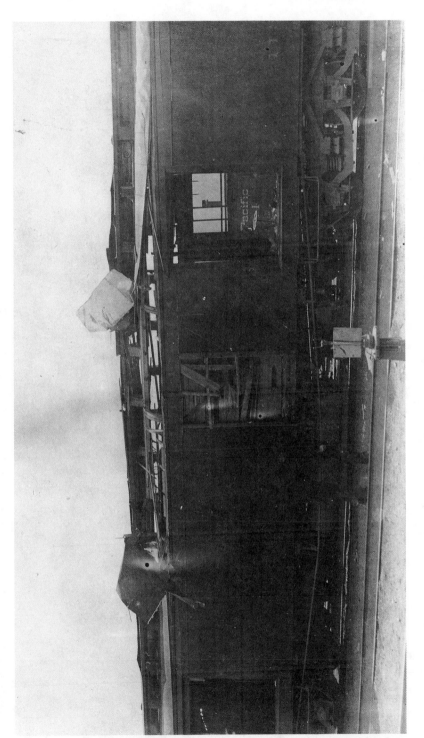

Exterior view of Express car blown up at Tipton, Wyoming, August 29, 1900 (Courtesy Union Pacific Railroad.)

Posse which trailed the "Wild Bunch." 1. George Hiatt, 2. T.T. Kelliher, 3. Joe Lefores, 4. H. Davis, 5. Si Funk and 6. Jeff Carr. (Courtesy Union Pacific Railroad, 101.)

Another picture of the posse that trailed the Wild Bunch. (Courtesy Union Pacific Railroad,103.)

Wild Bunch posse loading on train to go after the gang (Courtesy Union Pacific Railroad, '50.)

Interior view of the posse on a special train provided by the Union Pacific Railroad to track the Wild Bunch (Courtesy Union Pacific Railroad, 102.)

Rangers (Chief of their special car posse); U.S. Marshal Frank Hadsell; Sheriff McDaniels of Carbon County; Sheriff Swanson of Sweetwater County; and U.S. Deputy Marshal Joe LeFors. Two weeks after the robbery, the posses were still chasing them towards Colorado Territory.[9] Mr. LeFors tracked them as far as the Little Snake River near Baggs, Wyoming, where some money wrappers were found.[10]

The wrappers were evidence that Mr. Woodcock's quote of $55,000 was more accurate than the Union Pacific claim of $50.40. It was rumored at the time that the gang had been told a large gold shipment would be on board but it was apparently on another train. They did, however, get four packages from the mailbags which contained jewelry and watch parts. One 14K gold and diamond ring alone was reportedly worth $89.59 in 1890.[11]

It was said that the robbers were Sundance, Butch Cassidy, Harvey Logan (Kid Curry), and two others. The other names mentioned as participants vary, but they included Ben Kilpatrick, his girlfriend Laura Bullion, O.C. *Deaf Charley* Hanks, William Cruzan, and Bill Carver. However, Sundance was not there.

After the robbery, two friends of Sundance were questioned by the Pinkertons. Jim Ferguson, of the Snake River area, and John P. Ryan, of Rawlins, Wyoming, both made statements.[12] (Ferguson had even supplied Harvey Logan with a horse for the robbery. A posse later recovered it and described it as *Brown: star on forehead, snip nose, has pothook right shoulder, white left hind foot inside*.[13]) In their statements to the Pinkertons, Ferguson and Ryan were contacts between Sundance and a Bob Cruzan, who was in the Rawlins area with Harvey Logan prior to the robbery. About ten days before the robbery, Ferguson told Ryan, *Tell Bob*

(that) Harry Alonzo says he cannot be at that place.
Harry Alonzo was an often used alias of Sundance's. The
Pinkerton notes even suggested that both Ferguson and
Ryan *should be arrested as accessory before and after the
fact*, based upon their statements.[14]

In fact, the Pinkerton *Criminal History* on
Sundance further reads, *In August 1900 Longbaugh
(sic) agreed to take part in a train robbery on the Union
Pacific road with Harvey Logan, but mean while having
met Butch Cassidy he decided to go with Cassidy to
Nevada and sent word to Logan by Jim Ferguson he
could not keep his appointment..* [15]

For years researchers have wondered how the
gang could have been at Tipton, escaped to the south,
evaded a posse, crossed mountains and rivers, and still
managed to arrive outside Winnemucca, Nevada, (about
600 miles away) in less than two weeks. The horses and
the men would have been played out. Although Sundance
may have later been allotted a share of the Tipton
proceeds, he arrived in Winnemucca with a clear con-
science as far as Tipton was concerned.

Notes

1. Pinkerton files, undated Tipton report.
2. *Daily Pottstown Ledger*, August 31, 1900.
3. Baker, op cit, page 191.
4. *The Cheyenne Leader*, August 31, 1900; *Daily Pottstown Ledger*, August
   31, 1900, and September 7, 1900.
5. *Wyoming State Tribune*, August 31, 1900.
6. *Daily Pottstown Ledger*, August 31, 1900.
7. *The Cheyenne Leader*, August 31, 1900.
8. *Daily Pottstown Ledger*, August 31, 1900.
9. *The Cheyenne Leader*, August 31, 1900.
10. Kirby, op cit, page 80.
11. Kelly, op cit, page 275.
12. Pinkerton files, undated Tipton report.
13. *Ibid*.
14. *Ibid*.
15. *Ibid*, Denver Office History.

Pinkerton's National Detective Agency.

FOUNDED BY ALLAN PINKERTON, 1850.

MAY 20 1901

ROBT. A. PINKERTON, **New York,**
WM. A. PINKERTON, **Chicago,** } Principals.

GEO. D. BANGS,
General Superintendent, New York.
ALLAN PINKERTON,
Asst. to Principals and Gen'l Supt.,
New York.

JOHN CORNISH, Ass't Gen'l Sup't., Eastern Division, New York.
EDWARD S GAYLOR, Ass't Gen'l Sup't., Middle Division, Chicago.
JAMES McPARLAND, Ass't Gen'l Supt., Western Division, Denver.

Attorneys:—GUTHRIE, CRAVATH & HENDERSON,
New York

TELEPHONE CONNECTION.

OFFICES.

DENVER, OPERA HOUSE BLOCK.
J. C. FRASER, Sup't.
NEW YORK, 57 BROADWAY
BOSTON, 30 COURT STREET
PHILADELPHIA, 441 CHESTNUT STREET
MONTREAL, MERCHANTS BANK BUILDING
CHICAGO, 201 FIFTH AVENUE
ST. PAUL, GERMANIA BANK BUILDING.
ST. LOUIS, WAINWRIGHT BUILDING.
KANSAS CITY, 622 MAIN STREET.
PORTLAND, ORE. MARQUAM BLOCK.
SEATTLE, WASH. BAILEY BLOCK.
SAN FRANCISCO, CROCKER BUILDING

Representing American Bankers Association.

$6,000 REWARD

THE FIRST NATIONAL BANK OF WINNEMUCCA, NEVADA, a member of THE AMERICAN BANKERS' ASSOCIATION, was robbed of $32,640 at the noon hour, September 19, 1900, by three men, who entered the bank and held up the cashier and four other persons. Two of the robbers carried revolvers and the third a Winchester rifle. They compelled the five persons to go into the inner office of the bank, where the robbery was committed.

At least $31,000 was in $20 gold coins; $1,200 in $5 and $10 gold coins; the balance in currency, including one $50 bill.

THE MEN WERE NOT MASKED AND CAN BE IDENTIFIED.

The robbers are described as follows:

No. 1 (who entered the cashier's office and forced him, under threats, to open the safe).

AGE, about 35.
HEIGHT, 5 ft., 9 or 10 in.
WEIGHT, 160 pounds.
EYES, blue or gray.
NOSE, fairly long, but thin.
COMPLEXION, light.
HAIR, light flaxen.

BEARD, full, flaxen or blonde, and moustache light weight.
HANDS, (No. 7 glove) very small and much freckled on backs.
FEET, small.
OCCUPATION, probably cowboy.

Remarks: Walked as if lame at the hip. This may have been assumed. Has small veins, which show quite distinctly on globe of cheeks.

No. 2.

AGE, about 35.
HEIGHT, 5ft., 7 or 8 inches.
WEIGHT, 145 to 155 pounds.
BUILD, medium.

EYES, blue or brown.
HAIR, brown.
MOUSTACHE, moderately heavy, brown in color and drooping.

No. 3.

AGE, 25 to 30.
COMPLEXION, dark.
WEIGHT, 155 to 160 pounds.
BUILD, medium.

HEIGHT, 5ft., 9 or 10 inches.
EYES, dark brown.
FACE, smooth.

Remarks: Very determined expression in face. Smelled like a polecat. Think his hair was colored for the occasion. Two of the bank employes say he had a scar on one side of cheek, something like a wrinkle or life line.

Early Pinkerton reward poster for the Winnemucca bank robbery. (Courtesy Pinkerton Detective Agency.)

Chapter Sixteen

Winnemucca

September 19, 1900

Winnemucca, Nevada was called French's Ford in 1850, and served as a trading camp on the crossing of the Humboldt River. In 1867 the Central Pacific Railroad brought new prosperity to the area along with a new name honoring a local Piute Indian Chief.[1]

Today Winnemucca is a small city, specializing in vacations for gamblers. It is easily reached on Interstate 80, only 164 miles east of Reno.

Back in 1900, Winnemucca laid claim to a robbery by Sundance, Butch Cassidy, and the rest of the Wild Bunch. In spite of the almost constant debate concerning many of the robbery particulars, every September the town holds its *Butch Cassidy Days* and reenacts this most famous of the Wild Bunch robberies.

In early September of 1900, Sundance had skipped Tipton and ridden west from Wyoming, scouting the area along the way. He stopped in Battle Mountain, Nevada, to purchase four extra horses.[2] (The fact that he purchased four and not three horses is elemental in explaining one of the theories for Butch Cassidy's participation in this robbery. This theory is discussed later in the chapter.) As he continued west, he boarded his four grey horses at the Silve Ranch, about 30 miles northeast of Winnemucca.[3]

129

The original Winnemucca National Bank Building.
(Courtesy Sundance Properties.)

On September 9, 1900, Sundance, Harvey Logan (Kid Curry), and Bill Carver made camp in one of the sections of the George D. Bliss C S Ranch, about 14 miles east of Winnemucca. They chose a field bordering the old Sloan Ranch, near a haystack and a well. The C S Ranch Superintendent was F.J. Button, whose ten year-old son was named Vic.[4] Cowboys camping out after the area roundup was not new to Vic, but the outlaws had a fast and handsome white horse that fascinated him. Each day the white horse outran and outjumped Vic's horse.

During his visits, the men would ask the youngster about the town, the surrounding terrain, and the bank. Vic recalled in later years telling the cowboys about a shortcut from Winnemucca to Clover Valley via Soldier's Pass. In answering questions about the bank, Button also recalled telling one of the cowboys that Mr. Lee at the bank was a *crank*. One of the cowboys grabbed a big knife from his saddle and replied, *I'd just as soon stick him in the ribs*.[5] The knife-wielding cowboy was probably Harvey Logan, who had a reputation as a hothead with a penchant for violence.

The three cowboys remained camped just outside of town for the next ten days. Vic stopped by to admire the white horse and answer questions each day. One day the outlaw who rode the white horse promised to give him to Vic sometime. In later years Button always claimed this promise was made by Butch Cassidy, although he also said he never knew the names of the cowboys.

Beginning September 15th, Sundance, Carver, and Logan rode into town each day.[6] They rode through the town, past the bank, and became familiar with the entire area. For the next four days they stopped at a livery stable on the corner of Bridge and Second Streets, two blocks below the bank. There a fourth man joined them several times.

As the children left school for lunch each day, some of the boys often walked past the livery stable on their way to the Humboldt River. Nine-year old Lee Case remembered that these cowboys asked them questions about the town and the routes leading from town.[7] Case felt *they were just buckeroos*, like many of the roundup cowboys in town. For the next four days these young boys exchanged information for peppermint candy from the cowboys. Within ten days, the outlaws had gained useful information about the town, the bank, and the possible escape routes. A number of Winnemucca's young boys had also gained some fascinating memories.

On Wednesday, September 19, 1900, about noon, Sundance, Logan, and Carver tied their horses in the alley behind the F.C. Robbins and Co. store, next door to the bank. They walked around the buildings and entered the front door of the bank from Bridge Street. With revolvers drawn, they demanded that the bankers raise their hands.

While Sundance and Carver covered Assistant Cashier D.V. McBride, Bookkeeper Malvin Hill, and

Stenographer Calhoun, Harvey Logan kicked in the office door behind the counter.[8] Logan then also drew his knife and threatened Head Cashier G.S. Nixon and a horse buyer, W.S. Johnson, with instant death. Holding the knife to Nixon's neck, Logan had him open the vault safe and remove three bags of gold coins, worth about $5000 each.

Logan placed the bags of gold into an ore sack, along with loose money from the office cash drawer and the money from behind the counter. The outlaws reportedly stole $32,640 - *$31,000 in $20 gold coins, $1200 in $5 and $10 gold coins, with the balance in currency.*[9] The outlaws then marched all five hostages out the back of the bank into a fenced yard area just off the alleyway. The three outlaws jumped over the fence, ran up the alley, and mounted their horses. In less than five minutes they had completed their daring robbery.

Meanwhile, Nixon ran back into the bank, grabbed a revolver, and ran out the front door. Shooting into the air, he began to sound the alarm that the bank had been robbed. Johnson also grabbed a *pumping gun* and fired after the fleeing outlaws, only to find the rifle was not loaded.[10] Sundance and the gang raced down the alley to Second Street and turned right. As they then crossed Bridge Street, they shot a few rounds up towards the crowd gathering around Nixon.

A number of townspeople gave chase on foot, and even bicycle, as far as they could. The outlaws took a shot at Sheriff Charles McDeid as he came out of the Reception Saloon on Second Street. An elderly man named Chris Lane was shot at when he came out of his home to see what all the noise was. Stenographer Calhoun, on his way across town towards the hospital, was stopped in his tracks by the outlaws' gunfire. With all the shooting, however, no one was injured.[11]

The outlaws continued down Second Street towards the Golconda Road, and across the Cross Creek Bridge. McDeid and Calhoun were near the bridge, opposite each other, when they saw one of the robbers drop a sack of gold coins. Handing his reins to a pal, the thief jumped down, retrieved the sack, and the robbers all galloped off in a northeasterly direction.[12]

Deputy Sheriff George Rose climbed a nearby windmill to see their escape route. When he climbed down, Rose and a few others ran to the nearby siding where a Southern Pacific switch engine was parked. Although the engine had to build up steam and Rose had to stop for permission to gain access to the main railroad line, the engine quickly closed the gap on the thieves. The train tracks followed the river and the Golconda Road, along which the outlaws were racing. The townsmen opened fire and wounded one of the horses.[13]

Near Buttons Point (at exit 187 on Interstate 80 today) the outlaws turned away from the train tracks towards their campsite. The C S Ranch bordered the old Sloan Ranch, which was owned by the Winnemucca First National Bank. They were about 8 miles northeast of town, running hard, and riding a wounded horse. The outlaws stopped and took two horses, including a big black that belonged to Head Cashier Nixon. Two worn out horses were left behind as the bank robbers raced for the short cut to Clover Valley through Soldier's Pass.[14]

Nixon immediately wired neighboring Golconda, Nevada. The Golconda posse misunderstood the direction the outlaws took and failed to cut off their escape route. Instead, the Golconda men met the Winnemucca posse and joined in the chase.[15] Telegrams were sent out for posses from Boise City, Idaho; Silver City, Idaho; Burns, Oregon; Vale, Oregon; and Ontario, Oregon.

A posse was not necessarily a large number of lawmen. Six different posses are mentioned, three from

Pinkerton's National Detective Agency.

OFFICES.

FOUNDED BY ALLAN PINKERTON, 1850.

DENVER, OPERA HOUSE BLOCK.
JOHN C. FRASER, Resident Sup't.

ROBT. A PINKERTON, New York,
WM. A. PINKERTON, Chicago, } Principals.

GEO. D. BANGS,
General Manager, New York.
ALLAN PINKERTON,
Assistant General Manager
New York

JOHN CORNISH, Manager, Eastern Division, New York.
EDWARD S. GAYLOR, Manager, Middle Division, Chicago.
JAMES McPARLAND, Manager, Western Division, Denver.

Attorneys:—GUTHRIE, CRAVATH & HENDERSON,
New York. TELEPHONE CONNECTION.

NEW YORK, 57 BROADWAY.
BOSTON, 30 COURT STREET.
MONTREAL, MERCHANTS BANK BUILDING.
BUFFALO, FIDELITY BUILDING.
PHILADELPHIA, 441 CHESTNUT STREET.
PITTSBURGH, SECOND NAT'L BANK BLDG
CLEVELAND, GARFIELD BUILDING.
CHICAGO, 201 FIFTH AVENUE.
ST. PAUL ERNST BUILDING.
ST. LOUIS, WAINWRIGHT BUILDING.
KANSAS CITY, 622 MAIN STREET.
OMAHA, NEW YORK LIFE BUILDING.
PORTLAND, ORE. MARQUAM BLOCK.
SEATTLE, ARCADE BUILDING.
SPOKANE, PEYTON BUILDING.
LOS ANGELES, BRYSON BUILDING.
SAN FRANCISCO, CROCKER BUILDING

REPRESENTING THE AMERICAN BANKERS' ASSOCIATION.

$2,000.00 REWARD.

CIRCULAR No. 3.

DENVER, Colo., November 14th, 1904.

THE FIRST NATIONAL BANK OF WINNEMUCCA, Nevada, a member of THE AMERICAN BANKERS' ASSOCIATION, was robbed of **$32,640** at the noon hour, September 19th, 1900, by three men who entered the bank and "held up" the cashier and four other persons. Two of the robbers carried revolvers and a third a Winchester rifle. They compelled the five persons to go into the inner office of the bank while the robbery was committed.

At least **$31,000 was in $20 gold coin ; $1,200 in $5 and $10 gold coin ;** the balance in currency, including one $50 bill.

Since the issuance of circular No. 1, dated Denver, Colo., May 15th, 1901, and circular No. 2, dated Denver, Colo., February 3rd, 1902, it has been positively determined that two of the men who committed this robbery were:

1. GEORGE PARKER, alias "**BUTCH**" **CASSIDY,** alias **GEORGE CASSIDY,** alias **INGERFIELD.**

2. HARRY LONGBAUGH, alias "**KID**" **LONGBAUGH,** alias **HARRY ALONZO,** alias "**THE SUNDANCE KID.**"

PARKER and LONGBAUGH are members of the HARVEY LOGAN alias "KID" CURRY band of bank and train (express) "hold up" robbers.

For the arrest, detention and surrender to an authorized officer of the State of Nevada of each or any one of the men who robbed the FIRST NATIONAL BANK OF WINNEMUCCA, the following reward is offered by THE FIRST NATIONAL BANK OF WINNEMUCCA :

$1,000 FOR EACH ROBBER. ALSO 25 PER CENT., IN PROPORTIONATE SHARES, ON ALL MONEY RECOVERED.

Persons furnishing information leading to the arrest of either or all of the robbers will be entitled to share in the reward.

Later Pinkerton reward poster (Courtesy Union Pacific Railroad)

Below appear the photographs, descriptions and histories of GEORGE PARKER, alias "BUTCH" CASSIDY, alias GEORGE CASSIDY, alias INGERFIELD and HARRY LONGBAUGH alias HARRY ALONZO.

GEORGE PARKER.
First photograph taken July 15, 1894.

Name . . George Parker, alias " Butch " Cassidy, alias George Cassidy, alias Ingerfield.
Nationality . . . . American
Occupation . . . . Cowboy ; rustler
Criminal Occupation . . . . . . Bank robber and highwayman, cattle and horse thief
Age . . 36 yrs. (1901) . . *Height* . . . . 5 feet 9 in
Weight . . 165 lbs. . . . . . *Build* . . . . Medium
Complexion . . Light . . *Color of Hair* . . Flaxen
Eyes . . . . Blue . . . . *Mustache* . Sandy, if any
Remarks :—Two cut scars back of head, small scar under left eye, small brown mole calf of leg. " Butch " Cassidy is known as a criminal principally in Wyoming, Utah, Idaho, Colorado and Nevada and has served time in Wyoming State penitentiary at Laramie for grand Larceny, but was pardoned January 19th, 1896.

GEORGE PARKER.
Last photograph taken Nov. 21, 1900.

HARRY LONGBAUGH.
Photograph taken Nov. 21, 1900.

Name . . . . Harry Longbaugh, alias " Kid " Longbaugh, alias Harry Alonzo alias Frank Jones, alias Frank Boyd, alias the " Sundance Kid."
Nationality . . . . Swedish-American . . *Occupation* . . . . Cowboy ; rustler
Criminal Occupation . . . . Highwayman, bank burglar, cattle and horse thief
Age . . . . 35 years . . . . *Height* . . . . 5 feet 10 in
Weight . . . . . . 165 to 175 lbs. . . . . *Build* . . . . Good
Eyes . . . . . . Blue or gray . . . . *Complexion* . . . . Medium
Mustache or Beard . . . . (if any), natural color brown, reddish tinge
Features . . . . . . Grecian type . . . . *Nose* . . . . Rather long
Color of Hair . . . . Natural color brown, may be dyed ; combs it pompadour
IS BOW-LEGGED AND HIS FEET FAR APART.
Remarks :—Harry Longbaugh served 18 months in jail at Sundance, Cook Co., Wyoming, when a boy, for horse stealing. In December, 1892, Harry Longbaugh, Bill Madden and Henry Bass " held up " a Great Northern train at Malta, Montana. Bass and Madden were tried for this crime, convicted and sentenced to 10 and 14 years respectively ; Longbaugh escaped and since has been a fugitive. June 28, 1897, under the name of Frank Jones, Longbangh participated with Harvey Logan, alias Curry, Tom Day and Walter Putney, in the Belle Fourche, South Dakota, bank robbery. All were arrested, but Longbaugh and Harvey Logan escaped from jail at Deadwood, October 31, the same year. Longbaugh has not since been arrested.

☞ Officers are warned to have sufficient assistance and be fully armed, when attempting to arrest either of these outlaws, as they are always heavily armed, and will make a determined resistance before submitting to arrest, not hesitating to kill, if necessary.

☞ This circular cancels circulars No. 1 and 2, issued by us from Denver, Colo., May 15th, 1901 and February 3rd, 1902, respectively.

IN CASE OF AN ARREST immediately notify PINKERTON'S NATIONAL DETECTIVE AGENCY at the nearest of the above listed offices.

Or

Pinkerton's National Detective Agency,

JOHN C. FRAZER,   Opera House Block, Denver, Colo.

Resident Sup't., DENVER, COLO.

Winnemucca, and one each from Elko County, Golconda, and Tuscarora.[16] The main posse consisted of Deputy Sheriff George Rose, Roy Trousdale, Edward A. Drucker, James Hurst, Ernest A. Duvivier, and Ed Cavanaugh. Each of the other posses consisted of only three or four men who rode only a day or two each. The likelihood of actually apprehending the outlaws was only a remote possibility.

The Winnemucca and Golconda posses took off in pursuit of the trio as they continued heading northeast towards Tuscarora. About 3 p.m. the outlaws galloped into the Silve Ranch, nearly thirty miles from the bank. Sundance had left four greys at the Silve Ranch and paid the foreman, Silvian Siard, to care for them. Siard thought Sundance was a cattle buyer.

During the next hour, the outlaws carefully packed their loot and provisions onto one of the horses, saddled their new mounts, and rested their tired horses. They were about to leave around 4 p.m. when the posse was seen in the distance. A ranchhand wondered aloud what was happening, and one of the outlaws answered that it was a posse who was chasing them for the Winnemucca Bank robbery. He told the ranch hand to tell the posse it would be *unhealthy* for them to follow.[17]

It was at this time that the white horse was left behind.[18] As they were riding out, one of the outlaws told the ranch hand to give the white horse to the kid at the C S Ranch. Upon later examination, Vic found that nearly all the hair had been worn off on one side of the horse's neck, possibly due to the heaviness of the sack of gold coins rubbing there.

The posses nearly caught up with Sundance, Carver, and Logan because of this relay change. One of the Golconda men, an Indian tracker, got within a couple hundred yards of the gang. They raced parallel for a distance, and then one of the outlaws dismounted and aimed his rifle at the pursuing Indian.[19] Recognizing he was in danger, the Indian dropped back to await the rest of the posse and allowed the outlaws to escape. No actual shots were fired.

Shortly after nightfall, the outlaws passed the Clover Valley Cattle Ranch. The posse arrived later that night. Their horses were thoroughly winded, so they were forced to stop at the ranch for the night. In the morning most of the posse members returned to their homes, while the others took off with fresh mounts.[20] They soon came upon a campsite in Squaw Valley, where the outlaws had obviously divided the loot. Money wrappers and coin sacks were strewn all over the area, and the extra horses had been turned loose.

At 3:05 p.m. Thursday, September 20th, Sheriff Charles McDeid, who had remained in Winnemucca, received a telegram, from Ernest A. Duvivier, then in Tuscarora. It read, *Bank robbers are twelve miles from here. They are headed for White Rock and if all ranchers north of here are notified they can be captured. Their horses are worn out. Ed Cavanaugh and Burns Colwell are with me.* [21] Colwell was the Constable with the Golconda posse.

The previous day, Tuscarora had refused to organize a posse unless all expenses would be guaranteed. By the time this was authorized, it was too late to send a posse out to intercept the outlaws. When a posse was later raised, it only checked a few sheep camps in the area.[22] A camp near Sunflower Flat, thirty miles from Tuscarora, was found to have been raided, but it was thought to be a decoy by an accomplice.[23] Only provisions and ammunition had been taken, and a rifle had been broken and left behind. (This was likely done by the missing fourth man who was possibly Butch Cassidy. This theory is explained later in the chapter.) The Winnemucca newspaper sarcastically wrote, *If the*

Tuscarorans had acted as they should have done the desperadoes would now be in custody.[24]

A local historian, Antoine Primeaux, told me that the gang had taken the shoes off their horses in Midas, just west of Tuscarora.[25] This confused the posse, and they eventually lost the trail of the outlaws. When the outlaws came into Tuscarora later that day, Dr. Frank Drake, a friend of Primeaux's, recognized them as the three men who were previously in the area. They were known as Bozeman, Stewart, and Hunter when in Elko, Nevada. Then on September 22nd, the Winnemucca newspaper reported that three men working in a wood camp in Tuscarora had not been seen since the robbery.[26] One had been last seen the previous Monday riding a grey horse like the one used in the Winnemucca holdup. No identities were yet known even though no masks had been worn during the robbery.

Sundance, Carver and Logan continued heading for Owyhee, Nevada, a wild and inaccessible area known as the Junipers, on the Nevada-Idaho border.[27] Today, it is on the Duck Indian Reservation on State Route 225. By Friday morning, September 21st, they were over thirty miles past Tuscarora. That night they reportedly passed near Harvey Rutherford's Ranch, thirty-six miles east of Tuscarora and over 100 miles east of Winnemucca. By the 23rd, the posses stopped at Mrs. Johnson's Station in North Fork, a small town near the Rutherford Ranch, obviously falling farther and farther behind the outlaws. Here the posse from Elko County joined the chase, but all indications were that the robbers had escaped through the Junipers into Idaho. It was then assumed that the gang would head for freedom in the Jackson Hole, Wyoming, area. In spite of this, Winnemucca newspapers still claimed their capture was imminent.

With rewards worth over $10,000 on their heads, Sundance, Logan, and Carver (and the possible fourth, Butch Cassidy) made another clean escape. Logan and Carver both went directly to Texas. Sundance headed west to California, where he visited his brother, Elwood, in San Francisco. Researchers ascribing Butch Cassidy as the fourth man believed that Butch went east towards Wyoming. The four eventually met in Fort Worth, Texas.

The newspaper reports got smaller and more repetitive with each day. The last article of any length was on September 27, 1900.[28] By then two of the outlaws were believed to be a Melville Fuller of White Rock and a sheep shearer named Perkins. Over the next few months other names surfaced and were disposed of methodically.[29] The third outlaw was then said to be Willie Wier, but these were all local men whose faces should have been recognized. Two other local men suspected were March Fuller, Melville's brother, and a French sheepherder named Francis Silve. According to town rumors, a Charlie Craig was implicated by Perkins; but when he was captured in Idaho, Nixon went to identify him and did not recognize him. Any of these men could have been local accomplices, but no charges were ever brought against them.

The only other suspect to surface was also implicated by Perkins, according to town rumor. This man was known as Dave Jones.[30] Nixon carefully checked Jones out and discovered that he had also been known as Frank Jones. Nixon even obtained a check which Frank Jones had endorsed in payment for a horse, and the signature matched that of Dave Jones. The alias Frank Jones was often used by Sundance. Nixon himself claimed that one of the outlaws was called *Alonzo,* further evidence that Sundance participated in the Winnemucca robbery. In a later letter to the Pinkertons,

Nixon identified Sundance as being the man known as Harry Alonzo.[31]

This robbery was possibly the most famous and most familiar because of the photograph of these members of the Wild Bunch which was taken in Fort Worth, Texas, after the robbery. Tradition held that the picture was then sent back to the bank in Winnemucca by the gang along with a thank you note for their new clothes. Today, the bank has an enlarged copy of this portrait in its lobby, but there was no evidence that an original was ever sent to the bank.[32] Another story was that the picture was sent to a town youngster, Vic Button, whom the gang had befriended. Button himself never claimed this to be true.

What actually happened was a Wells, Fargo & Company detective saw one of the original pictures in the photographer's studio and recognized Bill Carver, one of the gang.[33] He sent copies to fellow law officers for identification of the other men. He also sent one copy to the Pinkerton Agency. They sent a copy to George Nixon, Head Cashier of the Winnemucca Bank. They apparently hoped that he could identify some of the bank robbers. This was how the bank, through Nixon, became the owner of one copy of the photograph.

Researchers over the years have credited nearly every Wild Bunch member with this robbery. The most accepted list, however, includes Sundance, Butch Cassidy, Will or Bill Carver, and possibly Harvey Logan (Kid Curry). Herein lies two problems: the number and the names of the outlaws. Every newspaper and first-hand account of the robbery itself says that there were only three robbers. However, a number of young town boys who had seen the gang in town earlier said there were occasionally four men. The posses chased only three men, with no indication that a fourth ever joined their escape. So, who was the fourth outlaw and what happened to him?

At that time of the year, many extra cowboys were in the area because it was roundup time. Roundup was when all the area ranchers got together to *round up* and brand all the cattle grazing on the open range. It was not unusual for a town such as Winnemucca to nearly double its adult male population during this time of the year. Therefore, the fourth man could easily have drifted in and out of town without causing suspicion, eventually drifting away without notice.

Butch Cassidy was often named as the fourth participant in the Winnemucca robbery. He was involved in the Tipton, Wyoming, train robbery on August 29, 1900. Tipton was over 600 miles east of Winnemucca. The land in between was extremely harsh, including alkali water holes, deserts, mountains, and a lack of helpful towns and ranchers. Butch might have been trying to evade a following posse. He would have found such a trip all but impossible to accomplish in time to set up camp by September 9, 1900; however, he could have been the fourth man who arrived just prior to the robbery.

Head Cashier Nixon continued to deny that Butch was one of the outlaws.[34] He claimed not to recognize Cassidy in the photographs sent to him. It was only after much pressure by the Pinkertons and five months time that Nixon wrote, *So far as Cassidy is concerned we will be willing to take chances in paying the reward for him upon the evidence now in hand . . . I am trying to get a description of Cassidy from a person who formerly knew him, as the photograph you sent me is the likeness of a man with a great deal squarer cut face and massive jaws, in fact somewhat of a bulldog appearance.*[35] He also reaffirmed what he had written in a previous letter, saying that, *while I am satisfied that Cassidy was interested in the robbery, he was not one of the men who entered the bank.*[36] One researcher, Lee Berk, wrote an article claiming Butch was not at Winnemucca. He concedes, however, that *Someone in the outlaw fraternity probably contacted Cassidy and sent the men who held up the bank.*[37]

That left Sundance, Carver, and Logan as the three outlaws involved in the bank robbery. In fact, Nixon and Assistant Cashier D.V. McBride both recognized *Harry Alonzo* (Sundance), Carver and Logan from the Fort Worth photograph as being the outlaws. Nixon further identified this same trio in a series of letters which he wrote to the Pinkertons.[38]

The last issue often debated concerns Head Cashier Nixon. George Stuart Nixon was already a successful, self-made young man from California by the time he settled in Winnemucca.[39] He quickly helped to form the First National Bank of Winnemucca, becoming part owner and Head Cashier. The President was Mr. F.H. Lee, and the Vice-President was Mr. J. Sibbald. In later years, Nixon went on to become not only a successful businessman and rancher, but also a member in good standing of the Nevada Legislature and eventually a United States Senator from Nevada.

The amount of money taken in nearly every robbery has been disputed with most victims/owners claiming less than their original quoted loss. This was done for the protection of the company reputation. With the Winnemucca robbery, however, the dollar value kept increasing. The first accounts reported that only three bags of gold coin, valued about $5000 each, were stolen, along with some gold from an office money drawer.[40] The total amount taken was said to be $15,000, with all silver and bank notes being left untouched.

Three days later a newspaper in nearby Elko, Nevada, quoted the amount taken as being, *three sacks* *of gold coin, each containing $5000 . . . together with all the gold coin in the office drawer, amounting to $6000 to $8000.*[41] So far, the take was up to about $23,000. Soon after the robbery, Nixon began writing letters to banking and law officials.[42] In September he wrote the federal government that $29,575 had been stolen. The next quote, from the local newspaper was $31,000. By December 9, 1900, Nixon told the Pacific Express Company that $31,640 was stolen; and on February 21, 1901, he wrote the Pinkertons claiming $32,640 was missing.

Due in part to this ever-increasing amount, a robbery setup was suspected, as cover for an inside embezzling job. Additional evidence for this came from a search of the outlaws campsite. Three letters were found, torn into small pieces. They were glued together and copies of all three letters were then sent to law officials and agencies. The letters also implied that the robbery was an inside job.[43]

The first letter was written on August 24, 1900, to *My dear Sir*. It carried the name and address of Douglas A. Preston, a Wyoming attorney who had befriended Butch Cassidy. The only sentence read, *Several influential parties are becoming interested and the chances of a sale are getting favorable.* The second letter had no heading, but the handwriting matched that of the first letter and was signed *P*. It said, *Send me at once a map of the country and describe as near as you can the place where you found that black stuff so I can go to it. Tell me how you want it handled — you don't know its value. If I can get hold of it first, I can fix a good many things favorable. Say nothing to any one about it.*

The final letter was dated September 1, 1900, and was written to C.E. Rowe of Golconda, Nevada. It read, *Dear Friend: Yours at hand this evening. We are glad to know you are getting along well. In regard to sale enclosed letters will explain everything. I am so glad that everything is favorable. We have left Baggs so write us at Encampment, Wyo. Hoping to hear from you soon I am as ever, Your Friend, Mike.*

The letter signed *Mike* was later identified as being written by a woman, further identified as Mrs. Mike Dunbar. Dunbar was a contact person for Butch Cassidy and was being watched by the Pinkertons.[44]

Alone, these letters seem innocent enough, but in the possession of the Winnemucca outlaws, they suggested to some lawmen that the robbery had been an inside job. Suspicion quickly focused on Nixon, who was certainly in a position to be the inside man.[45] To many this suspicion continues today. No one was ever able to identify C.E. Rowe either.

However, Nixon was the man who carefully pieced and glued these bits of paper in the three letters and forwarded them to the law enforcement officials. He certainly would not have done so if he were guilty of receiving them. As Head Cashier, Nixon was in a position to embezzle funds, but President Lee and Vice-President Sibbald were also in good positions with easy access to the banking funds. For that matter, so were the other cashiers. Evidence that the robbery was used to cover up missing funds is very strong, but no one person appears any more likely than the next.

Notes

1. Stanley W. Paher, *Nevada Towns & Tales*, Vol. I-North, 1981, Nevada Publications, Las Vegas, Nevada, pgs 170-171.
2. Kirby, op cit, page 81; Edward A. Drucker, "Witness Recalls Chasing Robbers," *The Humboldt Sun*, September 16, 1982, page 6c.
3. *Ibid.*
4. I. Victor Button, "Butch Cassidy Gave Getaway Horse to 10-Year-Old,"*Newsletter of the National Association and Center for Outlaw and Lawman History*, page 3.
5. *Ibid.*
6. Kirby, op cit, page 82-87.
7. *Ibid*, page 83.
8. Berk, op cit, page 11.

9. Pinkerton Files, Confidential Memo dated January 15, 1907, signed by Mr. Robert A. Pinkerton.
10. *The Silver State*, September 19 and 20, 1900.
11. *The Silver State*, September 20, 1900.
12. Toll, op cit, page 22, *The Silver State*, September 20, 1900.
13. Drucker, op cit, page 6c; *The Silver State*, September 20, 1900.
14. *Ibid.*
15. *The Silver State*, September 19 and 20, 1900.
16. *The Silver State*, September 19, 20, 21 and 22, 1900.
17. Drucker, op cit, page 7c.
18. *The Silver State*, September 20, 1900; Button, op cit, page 3.
19. *The Silver State*, September 20, 1900; Drucker, op cit, pages 6c and 7c.
20. *The Silver State*, September 27, 1900.
21. *Ibid*, September 20, 1900.
22. *Ibid.*
23. *Ibid*, September 27, 1900.
24. *Ibid*, September 20, 1900.
25. Author's interview.
26. *The Silver State*, September 22, 1900.
27. *Ibid.*
28. *Ibid*, September 27, 1900.
29. *Ibid*; Berk, op cit, pages 12-13.
30. *Ibid.*
31. *Ibid*; Pinkerton Files.
32. David W. Toll, "Butch Cassidy & The Great Winnemucca Bank Robbery," *Nevada*, May/June 1983, pages 21-27.
33. Dale L. Morgan, *The Humboldt, Highroad of the West*, published 1943, J.J. Little and Ives Company, pages 318-319.
34. Toll, op cit, page 26; Lee Berk, "Who Robbed the Winnemucca Bank?," in the *Quarterly of the National Association and Center for Outlaw and Lawmen History*, 1983, page 13.
35. Toll, op cit, page 26.
36. *Ibid.*
37. Berk, op cit, page 14.
38. *Ibid*, pages 13-15.
39. *Ibid*, page 15; Toll, op cit, page 27.
40. *The Silver State* (Winnemucca), September 19, 1900.
41. *The Free Press* (Elko), September 22, 1900.
42. Berk, op cit, page 13.
43. *Ibid*; Toll, op cit, page 24; Sheriff Frank Hadsell's private papers and correspondence in the Wyoming State Archives, Cheyenne.
44. Sheriff Frank Hadsell's private papers, H70-18/107-125, letter to Hadsell from Frank Murray of the Pinkertons and dated 3 December 1900.
45. Toll, op cit, page 27; Berk, op cit, page 15.

Wild Bunch photo taken in Fort Worth, Texas.

Chapter Seventeen

Texas Retreat

After the Winnemucca robbery, tentative plans were discussed for an escape to South America. Expense money was raised, and Sundance and Butch arranged to meet in Fort Worth, Texas, possibly for one last hurrah.

Fort Worth in 1900 was a frontier city in which someone with a reputation could easily lose himself in the crowds. A large portion of the city was built around the stockyards and the railheads, where herds of cattle were driven to Fort Worth to be shipped north by train. Cattlemen and cowboys made up a large percentage of its very transient population.

Bordered by 13th and 17th Streets between Main and Jones, Hell's Half Acre was a small, lawless city within the larger city of Fort Worth.[1] Today this entire area has been leveled and is a park and the city Convention Center, and Rusk Street is now Commerce Street.

Naturally, the entertainment and nightlife were aimed at pleasing all the men just off the range. These visitors were provided with taverns, gaming parlors, prostitutes, and a *safe* hideaway. In the middle of this area, at 1600 Calhoun Street, was a saloon run by a Mike Cassidy. This may have been the same Mike Cassidy who had influenced Butch when he was a young man, and the gang looked him up before they left the States.[2]

Fort Worth, Texas train station.
(Courtesy Sundance Properties.)

The beautiful Tarrant County Courthouse was built in 1894 and was certainly an impressive sight to Sundance and the others. One of the largest stores in town was the Parker-Lowe Dry Goods Store.[3] (I couldn't help but wonder if a certain Robert Leroy Parker liked the store name so well that he decided then to use the alias Jim Lowe.)

The Union Pacific Railroad depot was located at 15th and Jones Streets, south of the center of town. Sundance probably arrived from San Francisco by train in early November of 1900.

The remaining Wild Bunch members met here to say good-bye to Sundance and Butch before they went to South America. They must have had a grand time. One of their group, Bill Carver, decided to marry his sweetheart, Lillie Davis. Lillie had once been one of the Fannie Porter's girls in San Antonio, Texas. After the wedding, the whole gang held a big party in Maddox Flats at 1014 1/2 Main Street.[4] The idea for the photo may have begun at this party, perhaps to be a wedding momento.

On November 21, 1900, Sundance, Butch Cassidy, Bill Carver, Ben Kilpatrick, and Harvey Logan sat for a photograph. They arrived at John Swartz's studio, located at 705 Main Street, decked out in their best clothes, including their derbys.[5] In later years, Swartz moved his studio to 503 1/2 Main Street.

The picture was a good example of his abilities, and Swartz put a copy of it on display in his studio. A Wells, Fargo & Co. detective named Fred Dodge happened upon it by chance and recognized one of the group as Bill Carver.[6] He asked for a copy to identify the others in the gang. It became the most famous photograph Swartz ever took. The Wells, Fargo & Co. office was located at 817 Main Street, just one block up from Swartz's studio.

Everyone again split up after their stay in Fort Worth. Harvey Logan and Ben Kilpatrick (The Tall Texan) headed north where they eventually met Butch Cassidy and held up the Great Northern train near Wagner, Montana. Bill Carver stayed in Texas and was killed by Sheriff E.S. Bryant in Sonora on April 2, 1901.

The others went to San Antonio for more partying at Fannie Porter's place. Both Fort Worth and San Antonio had a *red-light* district called *Hell's Half Acre*.[7] Fannie ran a house of prostitution in that area, and according to Pinkerton interviews she knew Butch. So Butch, Sundance and the remaining members of the Wild Bunch took this time to relax and possibly plan for the future.

Notes

1. Leonard Sanders, *How Fort Worth Became The Texasmost City*, published 1973, Amon Carter Museum of Western Art, Fort Worth, pages 77-85.
2. Selcer, op cit, page 319.
3. *Fort Worth Morning Register*, newspaper advertisements.
4. Sanders, op cit, pages 77-85.
5. Pinkerton Files; 1899-1900 *Fort Worth City Directory*, Fort Worth Public Library.
6. Pinkerton Files; Kelly, op cit, page 281; Toll, op cit, page 26.
7. Albert Curtis, *Fabulous San Antonio*, published 1955, The Naylor Co., San Antonio, pages 37-40.

The Sundance Kid & Etta Place (Courtesy The Pinkerton Detective Agency.)

Chapter Eighteen

Alias Etta Place

Few of the Wild Bunch members ever formed a long-term relationship with a woman; Sundance did. She was a complete unknown to authorities and many people have speculated about who she was.

The Pinkerton files most often referred to her as *Mrs. Longbaugh* or *Mrs. Place.*[1] However, they also called her by a variety of first names: Eva, Rita, Etta, and Ethel.

The first verified record of this woman was by the Pinkertons. They received a hospital report in May, 1902, which had a physical description of her. It read *Mrs. Harry A. Place, age 23 or 24, 5 ft 5. 110#. Med Comp Medium dark hair Blue or gray eyes regular features. No marks or blemishes.*

A memo written July 29, 1902 detailed her presence with Sundance in New York City in 1901. It referred to her as his wife. She remained *Mrs.* until a memo dated October 24, 1904, which referred to her as *Longbaugh's wife, Ethel Place.* Therefore, the first time she had a complete name, she was known as Ethel Place.

This information appeared when detectives discovered that a woman had accompanied Sundance when he first went to South America. They found the photograph which had been taken, possibly as a wedding momento. The family was told that they were truly married, although a marriage record has not been found. In all cases to that point, she was known only as the wife of Sundance, who was then using the alias of Harry A. Place. Therefore, she was referred to as Mrs. Longabaugh or Mrs. Place.

Continuing with the evolution of her name, the Pinkertons next found her signature. In their files today is a page from a register which bears the signatures *H.A. Place* and *Ethel Place*. Whether or not Ethel married Sundance, she took on his last name, which at the time was Place. Thus, Ethel Place came into existence.

She became better known as *Etta Place,* possibly because of the location in which she was discovered. By the time anyone knew of her presence with Sundance, Ethel was living in South America. In a Spanish-speaking country, pronunciation of a American name can change. Harry was called *Henrique,* the Spanish version of Harry. Likewise, pronunciation of Ethel was changed. In Spanish, there is no *th* sound, and an *l* at the end of the word is usually silent. Therefore, the name *Ethel* would be pronounced *Etta*. Detectives questioning the Argentine authorities were told, *Senora Etta Place* and they would hear and write *Etta Place*. By September 23, 1906, the name Etta Place was put into print, via a *New York Herald* newspaper article. The Pinkertons continued to refer to her by the name Ethel as late as January 15, 1907, when they released Circular #4, a wanted poster written in Spanish. However, as time went by and more reports came back from South America, the name Etta Place became more often repeated. It became a permanent fixture.

Beyond her name, this woman's background was also somewhat of a mystery. Some stories claimed Ethel was a school teacher, possibly a music teacher. She may have been a rancher's daughter; she was said to ride well and shoot straight when she participated in the South American robberies.

Nearly every Pinkerton record about Ethel suggests that she came from Texas. That may have been partly due to the fact that Sundance arrived in Texas alone but arrived in New York City accompanied by Ethel. There was some later speculation that she was from Denver, Colorado; however, a search in Denver proved empty.

Possibly the strongest evidence that she lived in Texas appeared in a letter written by William A. Pinkerton on May 12, 1906. Pinkerton wrote J.H. Maddox, Esq., the Chief of Police in Fort Worth, asking him *to try to learn through some of your acquaintances in Texas who this woman is and where she came from.* Frank P. Dimaio, the Pinkerton agent, wrote to author J.D. Horan on June 14, 1949, and stated, *She evidently had parents in Texas.* Dimaio further stated that, ... *my impression is that he may have met her in a house of ill fame ... but I have no personal knowledge.* Thus began the claim that Ethel was a prostitute, and possibly one of Fanny Porter's girls in San Antonio, Texas.

Fanny Porter lived at 505 South San Saba Street in San Antonio. She was born in England in February, 1873 and was a young widow. The 1900 census records list her as the *Head of Household* in a *Boarding House* with five young female boarders. However, none of the names of her five boarders even comes close to *Ethel.* The Pinkertons knew of Fanny and later interviewed her girls to no avail.

However, around the corner from Fanny's place, there was another well-known house at 212 South Concho Street. According to the 1900 census records, one of the residents in this *Boarding House* was Ethel Bishop, born in West Virginia in September 1876. Ethel was 23, single, and listed as an unemployed music

*Dan Breen Saloon circa 1905 on Houston
Street in San Antonio, Texas.*

teacher. Also living in this house with her were four
other young, single women: Jessie Sewall, 24, *Head of
Household;* Bessie Cummins, 20; Cora Laugel, 23; and
Pearle Wilson, 22, a *Coloured Housekeeper.* Ethel not
only lived in a house of prostitution, but she worked in
a *Class A House.*

(In 1911, *The Blue Book* was published by Elton
R. Cude. The preface reads, *This Directory of the Sporting District is intended to be an accurate guide to those
who are seeking a good time.* After a number of pages
with bar and saloon advertisements, page 5 states, *The
boundary of the Sporting District extends south on South
Santa Rosa Street for three blocks, beginning at Dolorosa
Street, thence from the 100 block to the end of the 500
block on Matamoras Street, thence from the 200 block to
the 500 block on South Concho Street, and lastly the 100
block on Monterey Street. This is the boundary within
which the women are compelled to live according to the
law.* On pages 21-27, there is a *Directory of Houses and*

Women which classifies them into A, B or C categories. Number 212 South Concho Street is listed as a Class A House, where one could spend the night, have his suit pressed by the housekeeper, and eat a hearty breakfast, as well as other amenities.)

Ethel Bishop was a prostitute in San Antonio in 1900; Etta Place was a prostitute from Texas. Ethel Bishop was an unemployed music teacher; Etta Place was said to have been a teacher, possibly a music teacher. Ethel Bishop did not appear in any city directory or census records after 1900, neither did she die or get married in San Antonio. Ethel Bishop just faded into obscurity about the same time Etta Place appeared on the scene because, this author believes, they were one in the same person.

The identity of Etta Place has always been a mystery. While none of the past theories to her background have ever been proven, we can add to the known facts a first name of Ethel. Whatever her name, she certainly brightened up the life of an outlaw, the Sundance Kid.

Notes

1. As indicated within the body of the chapter, all records have been supplied by U.S. Census Records, San Antonio City Directories as noted, family records, and the Pinkerton Files as shown. Further research shows Sundance was known to visit the Galveston, Texas area on numerous occasions, according to Sheriff Frank Hadsell's private papers, H70-18/107-125, Wyoming State Archives, Cheyenne, Wyoming, in a deposition from Bob Lee, taken on May 6, 1900, at the state penitentiary.

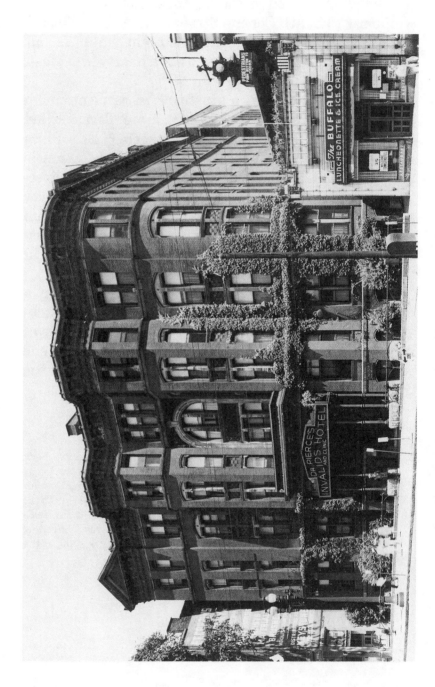

Dr. Pierce's Invalids Hotel. (Courtesy Buffalo and Erie

Chapter Nineteen

Pennsylvania Tourists

Sundance and Ethel left Texas in time to spend New Year's 1990-1 in New Orleans, Louisiana.[1] After their visit there, Sundance and Ethel headed north for a visit with his family.[2] They arrived in Pennsylvania at the same Phoenixville Railroad station that Sundance left from in 1882.[3] This was his first visit home in nearly twenty years.[4]

The station was within sight of his sister Samanna's home across the Schuykill River in Mont Clare. One can imagine them as they walked across the old covered bridge (which burned down in 1915) and turned left onto Jacob Street. Samanna's husband, Oliver Hallman, had his wrought-iron business next door to the house under the railroad overpass. When he was young, Harry spent many hours visiting with Samanna and Oliver.[5]

Sundance introduced Ethel as his wife to his brother, Harvey, and his sisters, Samanna and Emma.[6] He met his nieces and nephews, some born in his absence. Then he explained his decision to move to South America and told his family that he was going to settle down, buy a ranch, and go straight.

Because the Pinkertons were known to occasionally watch Samanna's house, Sundance and Ethel stayed

Samanna Longabaugh's home in Phoenixville, Pennsylvania. (Courtesy Sundance Properties.)

over in Phoenixville.[7] There were three hotels in town: the Mansion House Hotel, the Phoenix Hotel, and the Washington Hotel. The Mansion House Hotel was the closest to both Samanna's home and the train station.

The hotel, Samanna's home, and the railroad station are all still standing and in use today just off Route 29. Only the bridge has been replaced, although its location is still the same.

Sundance and Ethel visited the graves of his mother and father in the Morris Cemetery in Phoenixville. They toured the local sights that were a part of Harry's youth. They also visited with Harvey's family in nearby Flourtown and visited Emma's business, McCandless and Longabough, on Poplar Street in Philadelphia.

By mid January, 1901, Sundance and Ethel left the family in Pennsylvania and headed for New York City. William Pinkerton later complained in a memo to his brother Robert that while the Pinkertons were *look-*

Morris Cemetery, Phoenixville with markers of Josiah and Annie Longabaugh. (Courtesy Sundance Properties.)

ing for them in the mountains and wilderness out west, Sundance and Ethel were acting like New York tourists.[8]

Sundance told his family in Pennsylvania that he had sustained a pistol shot wound in his left leg while out west and would be seeing a doctor. A Pinkerton report indicates that both Sundance and Ethel checked into Dr. Pierce's Medical Institute in Buffalo, New York.[9]

In 1867 Dr. Ray V. Pierce founded the World's Dispensary Medical Association in Buffalo, New York. They made proprietary medicines such as Dr. Pierce's Golden Medical Discovery, Dr. Pierce's Favorite Prescription, and Dr. Pierce's Pleasant Pills.[10] The therapy and medications were a predecessor of today's holistic healing methods. (In June of 1907, Dr. R. Vaughn Pierce received a legal judgment of $17,581 from the *Ladies Home Journal* for making derogatory comments about his medication.)[11]

New York City. Building at left, West 12th Street, was the boarding house where Sundance and Etta spent three weeks. (Courtesy Sundance Properties.)

His business expanded to include the Palace Hotel, built in 1876 on Prospect Street. Photographs attest to a news article which described it as beautiful and grandiose.[12] However, a fire destroyed the hotel on February 16, 1881.

The Dispensary continued in the medicine business from their offices at 80 West Seneca Street while a new hotel was built. Dr. Pierce's Invalid's Hotel was opened at 653 Main Street in 1882, and by 1884 the Invalid's Hotel Annex was added at 655 Main Street.[13]

During the entire time Dr. Pierce continued to advertise his own medicines and treatments throughout the world. His patient list was said to have many international and well-known names, including President Coolidge. He used newspaper advertisements, barnside billboards, and testimonials which were part of a medical book he authored. Over a period of nearly 50 years, *The People's Common Sense Medical Advisor in Plain English* by R.V. Pierce, M.D., was printed in 100

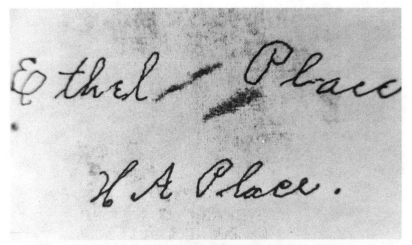

*Copies of signatures on file with The Pinkerton
Detective Agency. (Courtesy The Pinkerton
Detective Agency.)*

editions, each updated edition containing more testimonials.[14] More than three million copies were eventually printed and distributed worldwide, so it is understandable that Sundance and Ethel would have heard of this famous hospital.

Their advertised speciality was *treatment of all chronic diseases—particularly those of a delicate, obscure, complicated, or obstinate character*.[15] According to Pierce family members, the hospital records no longer exist. Therefore, the nature of Sundance and Ethel's health problems remains unknown.[16] Other researchers have speculated that the couple had a venereal disease. However, we also know that Sundance had a leg wound in need of treatment, and he had a severe catarrh (sinus) problem.

The Institute was a family-run business, with brother Dr. V. Mott Pierce a Harvard University graduate, second in command. At one time there were four doctors named Pierce on staff. By 1901 Dr. R. Vaughn

The DeYoung's Studio on Broadway at Union Square
where the photo of Sundance and Etta was taken.
(Courtesy Sundance Properties.)

Pierce was the president of the Institute and the Dispensary. In its heyday, the Institute employed over 100 people and served a capacity of up to eighty patients. However, by 1941 there were four doctors on staff serving only 30 patients, and the Board of Directors voted to close the Institute and to raze the old building.[17]

Today the address is in the center of the restored business and theater district, and the new business is a McDonalds. Next door is the Pierce building, a large office building built on the remaining property in 1921. Sadly, nothing remains of the once-famous medical and health spa facilities where Sundance and Ethel took Turkish baths and treatments.

Before they returned to New York City for their departure to South America, Sundance and Ethel went up to Niagara Falls, which was only twenty miles north of Buffalo. There they continued their recuperation.[18]

On February 1, 1901, Mr. and Mrs. Harry Place signed the guest register at Mrs. Catherine Taylor's boarding house.[19] Sundance and Ethel posed as a Wyoming cattle buyer and his wife. James Ryan (an alias of Butch Cassidy) was also registered there with them and passed as Ethel's brother.[20] The boarding house, located at 234 West Twelfth Street, had a second floor suite, which the trio rented for nearly three weeks.[21]

They visited all of the sights in New York City. Sundance and Ethel posed for a picture at the DeYoung Photography Studio, located at 826 Broadway, partly as a wedding momento.[22] That photograph became part of the Pinkerton files and appeared on many wanted posters. They also reportedly visited Tiffany's Jewelers on the corner of Fifteenth Street and Union Square, where Sundance bought Ethel a beautiful lapel watch for $150 and a diamond stickpin for himself.[23] They strolled often through the nearby park in Union Square and roamed past the outskirts of Greenwich Village.

Sundance and Ethel left for Buenos Aires, Argentina, on February 20, 1901. They purchased tickets for the British Ship *Herminius* under the names Mr. and Mrs. Harry Place.[24] Butch Cassidy went out west for one final robbery, in Wagner, Montana. Later, he met Sundance and Ethel in Argentina.

Notes

1. Kirby, op cit, page 88.
2. Pinkerton Files; Private Family Records
3. *Upper Providence Township 1805-1980*, history promotion booklet provided by Upper Providence Township offices.
4. Private Family Records.
5. *Ibid.*
6. *Ibid.*
7. *Ibid*; Kirby, op cit, page 95; Pointer, op cit, page 197; Pinkerton Files, undated Frank P. Dimaio Memo.
8. Pinkerton Files, letter to R.A. Pinkerton from Wm. A. Pinkerton dated July 31, 1902.
9. Pinkerton Files, memo to R.A. Pinkerton from Wm. A. Pinkerton, dated July 29, 1902.
10. *Buffalo Courier Express*, February 2, 1966.
11. *Buffalo Courier Express*, June 2, 1907.
12. *Buffalo Evening News*, July 2, 1978.
13. Pierce, R.V., M.D., *The People's Common Sense Medical Adviser in Plain English*, Ninety-Ninth edition, published 1914, World's Dispensary Medical Association, Buffalo, pages 923-925.
14. *Ibid.*
15. *1875 Buffalo City Directory*, Buffalo Public Library.
16. Interview April 28, 1992, correspondence with Pierce family.
17. *Buffalo Courier Express*, June 24, 1941; and *Buffalo Evening News*, June 23, 1941.
18. Private Family Records.
19. Pinkerton Files; Kelly, op cit, page 288.
20. *Ibid*; Pinkerton Files.
21. *Ibid*; Kelly, op cit, page 288; Kirby, op cit, page 88.
22. Pinkerton Files; Private Family Records.
23. Kirby, op cit, page 88 and 90; Kelly, op cit, page 288.
24. Kirby, op cit, page 93.

Part Three

February 20, 1901 — sailed to Argentina

April 3, 1902 — returned to the States

July 3, 1902 — Chicago - Rock Island train robbery

July 10, 1902 — returned to Argentina

1904 — returned to the States

February 14, 1905 — Rio Gallegos bank robbery

late 1905 — sold Cholila ranch; Chilean difficulties

December 19, 1905 — Villa Mercedes bank robbery

mid 1907 — working Concordia Tin Mines, Bolivia

May 1908 — Eucaliptus train robbery

August 1908 — Eucaliptus train robbery

November 4, 1908 — Aramayo mine robbery

GET CLEWS TO TRAIN ROBBERS.

Pursuers Believe Notorious Criminals Committed the Rock Island Holdup.

BAD MEN FROM THE WEST

Suspects Have Prison Records and Big Reward Hangs Over Their Heads.

The pursuit of the robbers who held up the Omaha and Denver express on the Rock Island road Thursday night near Dupont narrowed down yesterday afternoon to a search for two young men, believed to be experienced criminals, who lived in an Englewood rooming house for two weeks before the robbery.

A man who said he was well acquainted with the suspects during their stay in Englewood furnished the information to the Rock Island detectives. The suspects, he said, had not been seen there since Thursday afternoon.

Their descriptions correspond to the particulars given by the members of the train crew.

Bad Men from Out West.

In connection with the new clew the names

GEORGE PARKER.

HARRY LONGBAUGH.

*The **Chicago Tribune**, Sunday, July 6, 1902 article about the Rock Island train hold-up near Dupont, Illinois. The headline read "Suspects in Rock Island Train Holdup and Scene of Gun Fight With Farmers." (Courtesy Library of Congress.)*

Chapter Twenty

Going Straight
and then
A Return to Crime

The R.P. Houston Company ship *Herminius* arrived in Buenos Aires, Argentina, during the last week of March, 1901.[1] Mr. and Mrs. Harry Place disembarked and registered in the nearby Hotel Europa, a fashionable and popular hotel.[2]

They deposited 2000 pounds of Bank of England notes in the London and River Platte Bank in Buenos Aires, worth about $12,000 at the time.[3] They gave their residence as the Hotel Europa, again using the name Place.[4] Within two weeks and for the remainder of 1901, Sundance and Ethel toured the area, looking for land to purchase. By all indications, they meant to settle down on a ranch and live peaceful, law-abiding lives.

Within a year, Butch Cassidy joined them in Buenos Aires. Still using the alias James Ryan, Butch checked into the Hotel Europa on March 1, 1902, with Sundance and Ethel.

On April 2, 1902, Butch filed an application for *four square leagues of Government land within the Province of Chubut, district 16th of II October, near*

167

Cholilo . . . [5] He filed under the names James Ryan and Harry Place. A league, according to the dictionary, is *a measure of distance varying* . . . *usually about three statute miles*.[6] Researcher Larry Pointer said the ranch was on approximately 13,000 acres of land.[7]

Shortly after Butch arrived, Sundance and Ethel left for the States. On March 3, 1902, Sundance and Ethel boarded the S.S. *Soldier Prince*, of the Prince Line Ltd., and headed for the States. They arrived in New York City on April 3, 1902. They registered as Mr. and Mrs. Harry Place in a rooming house at 325 East Fourteenth Street.[8] A Mrs. Thompson was the landlady, although she was not the property owner according to the city tax records. According to a Pinkerton memo, Sundance and Ethel visited Coney Island, a popular beach and amusement park of the day.[9]

On this trip, Sundance and Ethel visited his family in Pennsylvania again.[10] Samanna's family remembered that Sundance told Samanna about the ranch Butch was preparing for all of them. He also invited her two sons to visit them in South America.

Sundance and Ethel also visited his brother Harvey, who lived in Atlantic City, New Jersey. Seven-year-old William Longabough played in the sand and surf with his Uncle Harry, and he passed that story on to his family in his later years.

An unidentified hospital report dated May 10, 1902 in the Pinkerton files read, *Harry Longbaugh (sic) alias Harry A. Place. About 35, 5 ft 9, 185 or 190. Med Comp. Brown eyes, Lt Bro hair. Lt Bro or Sandy Mustache (sic), feet Small. not bow legged — both feet turns in walking. face much tanned with the Sun. Mrs. Harry A. Place age 23 or 24 — 5 ft 5. 110#. Med Comp medium dark hair Blue or gray eyes regular features. No marks or blemishes.*[11] There was no indication of their treatment, although Samanna's family had been told that

Sundance had a gunshot injury to his leg, and that he was treated in a Chicago hospital.[12]

While in Chicago, Sundance apparently did more than have a medical checkup.[13] Around 11 p.m. on Thursday, July 3, 1902, the Chicago-Rock Island Railroad Express Number 5 was held up by two men near Dupont, Illinois.[14] Dupont was a small town about 17 miles west of Chicago; today it lies within Chicago's city limits.

A young man named Charles Nessler tried to steal a ride from nearby Englewood to his home in Rock Island and found two other men had hitched a ride in the same way. The two masked thieves forced Nessler to climb over the coal tender and tell Engineer Charles Goodall to stop the train. Goodall and his fireman, Albert Duckett, laughed at this *hobo joke* until Nessler convinced them to look up at the two gunmen behind them.

Once the train was stopped, the bandits used dynamite to force Express Messengers John E. Kain and William Reghal to open the doors of the car. Kain's footing slipped, and thinking he was trying to escape, one of the thieves shot him in the leg. Meanwhile Reghal had opened the smaller safe under threat of death and had removed a small amount of cash, some jewelry, and a few other items of lesser value. (Reports later place the total value at between $100 and $500.)

The outlaws quickly left with their small bag of loot, leaving about $90,000 in the larger safe untouched. A bag of dynamite was later found nearby, suggesting that they were prepared to blow the big safe but had left when some passengers became curious about the gunfire. They made their escape towards the northwest with horses and a wagon stolen from nearby farms. As many as 50 to 100 men were reportedly on the trail over the next week in pursuit of the train robbers.

Upon questioning by detectives, Nessler said the photographs of Sundance and Butch showed *a general resemblance . . . but the men had their faces covered.*[15] L.P. Moss, an area farmer, identified their photographs as the suspicious-looking men who had asked directions to Chicago. A hotel proprietor, J.W. Holstein, told the police of three boarders who were canvassing the area, one of whom *is said to resemble a photograph of Longbaugh (sic) the suspect.*

Holstein was not the only person to mention three outlaws. Reghal had told police he saw three men, and one posse reported three escaping in a team-driven wagon. The third outlaw could have been Ethel; she was known in later years to have participated in South American robberies.

Engineer Goodall claimed one of the thieves was bowlegged, which Sundance was, and various other descriptions matched both Sundance and Butch. Chicago Police Lieutenant Rohan described the thieves as *experienced train robbers*, and the *Chicago Record Herald* of July 5th stated it was *one of the best planned raids in recent years.*

In spite of the mounting evidence that Sundance participated in the robbery, doubt was expressed in the July 7th *Chicago Tribune.* However, no reasons were given for this doubt, and no one was ever captured for the holdup. Sundance had escaped once again.

Even the Pinkerton files include DuPont in a chronological listing of crimes perpetrated by the members of the Wild Bunch; full credit for the robbery is given to Sundance and Butch.

To arrive in New York in time for their steamer to leave for Argentina, Sundance and Ethel must have taken a train from Chicago. The man identified as Butch remains an enigma, as he could hardly have been in Argentina and Illinois at the same time.

Notes

1. Kirby, op cit, page 93.
2. Pinkerton Files, Frank P. Dimaio's notes of 1903.
3. *Ibid.*
4. Horan, op cit, page 261.
5. Kirby, op cit, page 95; Pointer, op cit, page 197; Pinkerton Files, Frank P. Dimaio's notes, undated.
6. *Webster's II New Riverside Dictionary*, published 1984, Berkley Books, New York.
7. Pointer, op cit, page 193-194.
8. Kirby, op cit, page 97.
9. Kirby, op cit, page 99.
10. Pinkerton Files; Kirby, op cit, page 97; Author's correspondence with Dan Buck and Anne Meadows, dated July 3, 1988; Private Family Records.
11. Pinkerton Files.
12. *Ibid*; Private Family Records.
13. Private Family Records.
14. *Chicago Record-Herald*, July 5, 1902; *The Chicago Daily Tribune*, July 5, 1902; *The Chicago Tribune*, July 6, 1902; *The Chicago Tribune*, July 7, 1902; two unidentified clippings in the Pinkerton Files.
15. All quotes are taken from *The Chicago Tribune*, July 6, 1902.

THE
EARLY WEST

Family photo of Sundance, Etta and Butch at Cholila

Chapter Twenty-One

Cholila Ranch
and
South American Crimes

On July 10, 1902, Mr. and Mrs. Harry Place sailed out of New York on board the steamer *Honorius*.[1] This ship, however, was a freighter, and did not have any passengers. Harry Place had hired on as purser, and Mrs. Place was listed as a steward. Researcher J.D. Horan claimed the Pinkertons had missed Sundance and Ethel in New York by only two weeks. They arrived in Buenos Aires on August 9, 1902, and checked into the Hotel Europa.[2] Sundance closed out his bank account on August 14, 1902, and he and Ethel left on board the S.S. *Chubut*, a steamer, for the ranch on August 15th. They went up the Gulf of Nuevo by boat and then traveled the remainder of the way by pack mule and horseback.[3]

This was not an easy trip. An undated and unsigned memo in the Pinkerton files states,

> *To reach it (the ranch) from Buenos Aires, would be by steamboat to Bahia Blanca, thence by smaller boat from Bahia Blanca to Rawson on the coast at the mouth of the Chubute (sic) River. From there on horseback to the 16 d'October district. Distance*

*Picture postcards of Cholila Ranch and Sundance,
Butch and Etta. (Copyright Paul D. Ernst.)*

*from Rawson to 16 d'October 200 miles, probably
two weeks travel. Fare New York to Buenos Aires
to Bahia Blanca and thence to Rawson $160 in
gold. Steamers run twice a month. Horse at Rawson
cost $50, wagon $200, provisions for two weeks
$100.[4]*

The trio set up their home in Cholila. They re-
sumed using their real names. Neighbors later described them as likeable, honest ranchers.[5] They were
active in local society and attended an inaugural ball for
the territial governor, Dr. Lezena.[6]

According to J.D. Horan's book, *The Wild Bunch*,
their ranch consisted of a large log building used as the
main house and a smaller bunkhouse used by the native
cowhands.[7] There was also a corral for their horses. The

Another picture postcard. (Copyright Paul D. Ernst.)

ranch was located in the Cholila Valley with a clear view of the area. As recently as 1992, the original ranch house was still standing, although it had a new roof and showed recent maintenance.[8]

Butch Cassidy wrote a friend in the States about their new home.[9] He said, *this part of the country looked so good that I located, and I think for good.* He went on to describe their ranch as having *300 cattle, 1500 sheep, and 28 good Saddle horses, 2 men to do my work, also good 4 room house, wearhouse (sic) stable, chicken house and some chickens.*

In late 1903 or early 1904, Sundance and Ethel returned for another visit to the States. A Pinkerton memo written on October 24, 1904, placed both Sundance and Ethel in the Fort Worth, Texas area.[10] (She may have been visiting her family this trip.) Earlier, they had

Cholila Ranch, circa 1903. (Copyright Paul D. Ernst)

Chapter Twenty-One

Cholila Ranch, 1992. (Copyright Anne Meadows)

*A third postcard with Etta, Sundance and dog
in front of the Cholila ranchhouse, circa 1903.
(Copyright Paul D. Ernst.)*

visited the 1904 St. Louis World's Fair and Exposition
and had sent a postcard to Sundance's sister, Emma. His
sister Samanna made only three more entries in her
diary and wrote her last letter to him on April 22, 1905.
This was possibly because Samanna wrote to Sundance
only while he was leading a law-abiding life. She continued, however, to hear from him on occasion, according to
her daughter-in-law.[11]

By all appearances Sundance and Ethel settled
down and enjoyed their lives as peaceful ranchers.
However, in 1905 things began to change for them. The
Pinkertons sent an operative, Frank P. Dimaio, into the
area to warn local authorities of their presence.[12] They
released wanted posters in Spanish into the Buenos
Aires and Cholila area.[13] They built a network of local
informants, including a neighboring rancher, Dr. George

Newberry, a dentist and an ex-vice consul from Buenos Aires. Their efforts to catch Sundance, Ethel, and Butch were so thorough, they even had a line of communication set up in code.

Using *Castleman, New York* as an opening, Newberry was to wire the Pinkerton Agency in code about a shipment of fruit. *Longabaugh = lemons, Cassidy = citron, L & wife = apricots. Mrs. L = peaches, L wife & Cassidy = oranges, sailed on = Pears.* Previous codes out west had named Sundance as *Sand* and Butch as *Primer.*[14]

An extradition treaty between Argentina and the United States was in existence at the time.[15] If any of them had been caught, they would have been returned to the States for trial. The risk of arrest was getting too high.

For this or possibly other reasons, they sold their ranch in Cholila around the end of 1905 to the Cochamo Company, a Chilean land company.[16] Their peaceful existence was ended.

They may have settled near the busy port city of Antofagasta, Chile, which would have provided them with anonymity in the large foreign population, easy access to the borders of other countries, and the availability of many ships sailing for distant shores. This was suggested by the interest of the Autofagastan authorities in verifying Sundance's death.[17] They may also have settled in Oruro, Bolivia, where Sundance, as Frank Boyd, was known to have been living in the *American Hotel*, according to an informant's letter written in 1909.[18]

Sundance and Butch returned to a life of crime. At 3 p.m. on Tuesday, February 14, 1905, the *Banco de Londres y Tarapaca* in Rio Gallegos, Argentina, was robbed by two English-speaking men.[19] The bank manager, Mr. Bishop, and the cashier, Mr. MacKareow, were forced to hand over 280 gold or sterling pesos and 23,000 paper currency pesos.[20]

Police later identified the *tall slight man and the other a shorter man, fair complexion, and both clean shaven* as being *Henry Linden and Co.*[21] The men had been staying at the Hotel Argentino in Rio Gallegos for about two months. The outlaws made a clean escape, heading towards the Patagonian Andes to the north.

Then on Tuesday afternoon, December 19, 1905, the Banco de la Nacion in Villa Mercedes, Argentina, was robbed by four American bandits. The armed outlaws escaped with 12,000 pesos.[22] On December 24, 1905, two Buenos Aires newspapers, *La Prensa* and *La Nacion*, each credited the Villa Mercedes robbery to the Sundance Kid, Ethel Place, Butch Cassidy, and Kid Curry.[23] (Harvey Logan, alias Kid Curry, was said to have joined the trio in South America about this time.) With amazing hindsight, the newspapers also credited the same group of bandits with the Rio Gallegos robbery earlier that year.

In the mid-1907's, Mr. Percy A. Siebert worked for the Cocordia Tin Mines in La Paz. In April, 1930 he told many stories of his association with Sundance and Butch to Mr. Arthur Chapman for an article he was doing for the Elks Magazine.[24] It was entitled *Butch Cassidy*, and recent findings have verified some of Mr. Seibert's stories. He told Mr. Chapman that beginning around mid-1907, Sundance and Butch began to work for the mines as payroll guards. They would leave on occasion, returning without explanation but with extra spending money. Mr. Siebert said they were robbing other area mines and banks, and using the Concordia as cover.

In May, 1908, two Americans held up the train station at Eucaliptus, Bolivia.[25] The thieves were believed to have been ex-employees, and they took about

15,000 bolivianos. The same two men were credited with another holdup on August 19, 1908, at kilometer 91, near Eucaliptus. In both instances, Sundance and Butch were later named as these unidentified American robbers.

As in the United States, many unsolved robberies were credited to the *Bandidos Yanqui,* Sundance and Butch. Much of the official information given by the police and newspapers was supplied by Frank P. Dimaio.[26] Therefore, the actual participation of Sundance, Ethel, or Butch in any robbery credited to them must be studied carefully.

Articles began to appear in papers in both the United States and in South America, many suggesting that Sundance was the leader of the gang. The *New York Herald* and the *Denver Republican* each printed an article on September 23, 1906, saying, *It is apparent that Longbaugh (sic), the leader of what is left of one of the most noted bands of robbers in this country . . .* [27]

On January 26, 1906, a Pinkerton memo issued in Philadelphia mentioned that Sundance was going by the name of Frank Boyd or H.A. Brown, and had been in trouble with the Chilean government *a short time ago.*[28] Because the memo was written in Philadelphia, it seems apparent that the mail from Sundance to his family was still being watched.[29] No reason for the trouble was ever found, but U.S. Vice-consul Frank D. Aller had assisted Mr. Boyd/Brown in clearing up the problem, at a cost of $1500. Mr. Aller worked for the American Smelting and Refining Company, located on Casilla 35 in Antofagasta, Chile.[30] He also earned a little extra money as an area consul, a political go-between or trouble-shooter for Americans in foreign countries. He may not have known Sundance's true identity when he helped him out of this difficulty with the Chilean authorities.

In the Buenos Aires newspaper, *Clarin*, articles written in 1907 by Justin Piernes reported that Sundance wrote a friend in Chubut, Argentina, around 1906. The letter said, *tomorrow we will leave for San Francisco . . . We have done well in business and we've received our money . . . I do not wish to see Cholila ever more.*[31] This suggested that Sundance and Ethel and possibly even Butch again returned to the States around 1906 or 1907. If they returned via San Francisco, it is likely that they visited with Elwood, Sundance's brother, who lived in San Francisco.[32]

On January 15, 1907, a Pinkerton memo stated that Sundance and Ethel were both living near Norquin, Province of Neuquen, Argentina.[33] This was apparently another ranch, since Cholila was not near Neuquen. But the 1907 date adds fuel to the idea that Ethel returned to South America with Sundance again after their San Francisco trip in 1906. Researchers Dan Buck and Anne Meadows feel that she continued to live with Sundance in Chile.[34] As evidence, they cite the correspondence between Mr. Frank D. Aller and the Charge d'Affaires, Alexander Benson, in La Paz, Bolivia. From 1909 through 1911, Mr. Aller was trying to verify the reported death of Boyd/Brown for someone in Chile, possibly Ethel.[35]

Other theories about Ethel said Sundance returned to the United States about this time because Ethel needed an appendectomy.[36] Another story said she returned to the States with Sundance because she was pregnant. Widower H.M. Elkins claimed his late wife Bettie Weaver had been the daughter of Ethel and Sundance, but he never proved this.[37] Both of these stories leave Ethel in a Denver hospital, to disappear forever. Meanwhile, a drunken, morose Sundance supposedly shot up the hotel in which he was staying before finally returning alone to South America.

On March 21, 1909 *Criminal informant, #85* filed a Pinkerton report in Los Angeles, California, in which he claimed to have spoken with Sundance in June of 1908.[38] The informant said they met at Villa de Mercedes.

He came in to see me from San Rafael, 100 miles southwest from there. Harvey Logan is with him there. They are in the cattle business and are owners of considerable land. They have a ranch some 40 miles in a southeasterly direction from San Rafael, down between the Atuel and Nuevo Salado Rivers and it is one of the finest stock countries on the globe.

San Rafael is quite a distance from either Cholila or Neuquen, so this appears to be yet another ranch.

The September 10, 1911, issue of *The Baltimore News* ran an article about Argentine outlaws. It read, *Shortly after Logan disappeared, Harry Longbaugh (sic) became the accepted leader of the outlaws.*[39] The gang was also called both the *Sun-Dance Kids* and the *Sun Dance Gang* in the article. Ethel was said to also be an active participant of this gang, wearing men's apparel and riding astride her horse.

Notes

1. Pinkerton Files, Frank P. Dimaio's 1903 notes; Kirby, op cit, page 97; Horan, op cit, page 262.
2. Pinkerton Files, Frank P. Dimaio's 1903 notes.
3. *Ibid*; Pointer, op cit, page 197; Kirby, op cit, page 100.
4. Pinkerton Files, Frank P. Dimaio's 1903 notes.
5. *Ibid*; also Frank P. Dimaio's report dated September 17, 1941.
6. Pointer, op cit, page 198; Justin Piernes, *Clarin*, "Butch Cassidy en la Patagonia," May 2, 3, and 4, 1970.
7. Horan, op cit, page 138.
8. Author's interview with Dan Buck, Anne Meadows, July, 1992.
9. Pointer, op cit, page 193, quoting letter to Mrs. Davis.
10. Robert A. Pinkerton Memo, October 24, 1904 .
11. Private Family Records.
12. Pinkerton Files, Frank P. Dimaio Report, September 17, 1941.

13. Pinkerton Files, Frank P. Dimaio's 1941 notes.
14. *Ibid*; unsigned notes in Folder 72, Binder 3.
15. Author's telephone interview with Dan Buck, June 27, 1988.
16. *Ibid*; *La Prensa* (Buenos Aires), January 26 and 27, 1906, as translated by Dan Buck.
17. South American research was done by Dan Buck and Anne Meadows. They were kind enough to share their findings and to translate the original newspaper clippings. All references to South American newspapers are as I received them. Other information from Buck and Meadows, "Wild Bunch Rampage in South America," in the *Quarterly of the National Association and Center for Outlaw and Lawman History*, Vol. XII No. 3-4, unless otherwise noted.
18. Pinkerton Files, memo dated January 26, 1906, initialed WJR; Bolivian Foreign Office Files from 1910, National Archives Records Office, in Washington, D.C.
19. *La Prensa* (Buenos Aires), February 16, 1905.
20. *Buenos Aires Herald*, February 16, 1905.
21. *Ibid*.
22. Buck and Meadows, op cit.
23. Pinkerton Files; *La Prensa* (Buenos Aires), December 24, 1905; *La Nacion* (Buenos Aires), December 24, 1905.
24. Horan, op cit, pages 273-290; Arthur Chapman, "Butch Cassidy," *Elks Magazine*, April 1930.
25. *La Prensa* (Buenos Aires), May 28, 1908, and August 25, 1908; Author's Correspondence with Buck, Meadows, October 1, 1988.
26. Pinkerton Files; Author's Correspondence with Buck and Meadows, July 3, 1988.
27. *The New York Herald*, September 23, 1906; *The Denver Republican*, September 23, 1906.
28. Pinkerton Files; unsigned memo dated January 26, 1906; Author's correspondence with Buck and Meadows, June 27, 1988.
29. Pinkerton Files, January 26, 1906, Memo, initialed W.J.R.
30. Bolivian Foreign Office Files from 1910, National Archives Records Office in Washington D.C.
31. Piernes, op cit.
32. Private Family Records.
33. Pinkerton Files, Confidential Memo from Robert A. Pinkerton, dated January 15, 1907.
34. Author's Correspondence with Buck and Meadows.
35. Bolivian Foreign Office Files from 1910, National Archives Records, in Washington, D.C.
36. Horan, op cit, page 282.
37. Author's correspondence with H.M. Elkins; Carl W. Briehan, *Wild Women of the West*, 1982, Signet Brand Western, 86-90.
38. Pinkerton Files, Memo dated March 21, 1909, detailing Informant #85 Reports, and initialed *H*, San Francisco, 4-5009.
39. *The Baltimore News*, September 1911; Letter to the Pinkertons from J. Cranstoun of Buenos Aires, dated January 8, 1910.

Chapter Twenty-Two

The Final Chapter

On November 4, 1908, two American bandits held up a payroll shipment near Tupiza in southern Bolivia.[1] The payroll belonged to the Aramayo, Francke & Cia Silver mines of Quechisla.[2] The two men escaped with 15,000 bolivianos (about $7000) and the pack mules which were branded with an A. By taking the mules, the outlaws left the mine administrator, Carlos Pero, his son, and a worker all stranded.[3]

Within hours, the company had alerted all the local authorities and sent out letters and telegrams. Contrary to the famous movie scene, a patrol of only three men happened upon the two outlaws as they rested for lunch in San Vicente, about 50 miles from Tupiza.[4] The patrol recognized the A on a stolen mule and asked local, armed miners to help. One newspaper reported a total of *5 or 6 armed men . . . a force of 6 men from the Abaroa Regiment.*[5] They further stated that within one hour a member of the posse and both bandits had been killed. The shootout in San Vicente, Bolivia, on November 8, 1908 went down in history.

The entire payroll amount was recovered, and the two unidentified bandits were buried as unknowns in the local cemetery. Over twenty years later, Percy A. Seibert gave names to these unidentified thieves buried as paupers in the small Bolivian village cemetery, even though he admitted to never actually seeing their bodies. He claimed the bandits had been Sundance and Butch.

Although a number of robberies had previously been credited to Sundance and Butch, all mention of their names seemed to have stopped shortly after the Bolivian shootout. The Pinkertons lost all track of them about the same time. While Pinkerton reports were still written and information occasionally exchanged, most was outdated. The Pinkertons were only too glad to close the books on the Sundance Kid and Butch Cassidy once Chapman's article came out.[6]

Over the years, many stories have surfaced, all built upon the premise that Sundance outlived the Bolivian shootout. He was said to have joined forces with Pancho Villa in the Mexican Revolution. Coincidentally, the Revolution began about the same time the South American reports ended.

Butch Cassidy's sister, Lula Parker Betensen, wrote a book about the return of her brother.

Ed Kirby's book tells of Hiram Bebee, a convicted murderer who died in prison in 1955. Ed felt that Bebee was Sundance, but the physical discrepancies are many. Harry Longabaugh Jr. always claimed his father, the Sundance Kid, died in Casper, Wyoming, in the 1950's. William Pinkerton wrote a memo about Butch and Sundance in which he thought that possibly Sundance was still alive in Chile as late as 1913.[7] In 1921, the Pinkertons thought Sundance was still alive, possibly in jail in Peru.[8] Numerous sightings were reported over the years, but again all remained unproven.

On July 31, 1909, Mr. Frank D. Aller, the Vice-consul in Antofagasta, Chile, wrote to the American Minister at the American Legation in La Paz, Bolivia. Aller was trying to verify the supposed death of Boyd/

Brown for someone in Chile.[9] Researchers Dan Buck and Anne Meadows believe this may have been an attempt to settle his estate.[10]

Mr. Aller wrote, *An American citizen named Frank Boyd is wanted in Antofagasta and letters addressed to him in Bolivia have failed to receive reply . . . The last address of Frank Boyd or H.A. Brown was 'American Hotel,' Oruro.*[11] Aller also stated, *I have been informed by Mr. Wm. Grey of Oruro, Mr. Thomas Mason of Uyuni (in San Vicente) and many others that Boyd and a companion named Maxwell or Brown were killed at San Vicente near Tupiza by natives and police and buried as 'desconocidos'.*[12]

Aller's attempts to obtain a death certificate, however, came to naught, as the Bolivian authorities answer was (roughly translated), *I also submit to you the death certificates of the two said persons whose identifications are not known.*[13] However, as late as January 21, 1911, Aller received a letter from the Bolivian authorities which included *a complete record of the case of Maxwell and Brown, drawn up by the authorities of the district where they were killed.*[14] This *complete record* is no longer attached to this letter, regretfully.

Finally, Sundance's sister Emma's 1918 will indicated that the family had not heard from Sundance for some time.[15]

Sundance's brother, Harvey, once told his son, Bill, that he had an uncle who died somewhere in South America; but he would not expand upon this information. Grandpop, Bill Longabough, died in silence before any of his descendants knew anything about an Uncle Harry.

The family was never able to verify Sundance's reported death in 1908. In the fall of 1991, author/researcher Dan Buck went with anthropologist Dr. Clyde Snow to examine the exhumed bodies of the outlaws involved in the shootout.

During the winter of 1991 and 1992, tests were run on the skulls and key bones. Comparisons were made using the Bolivian police files and inquest notes along with the known physical descriptions of Sundance and Butch. DNA testing for possible matching of genetic material was also done with descendants in Sundance's family.

As of this writing, Dr. Snow's research shows that the bullet wounds in the bones that were dug up match those described in the inquest papers. He further feels that the make-up of the key bones and skeleton match the known height and weight of Sundance. Finally, his computer super-imposition matching with the skull and known photographs of Sundance indicate the possibility of it being Sundance.

Bullet entry marks suggest that both men were badly wounded, and that Butch shot both Sundance and himself rather than to be taken. They had finally reached the end of their Outlaw Trail and found their hideouts were gone.

Notes

1. Buck and Meadows, op cit.
2. *La Prensa* (Buenos Aires), November 7 and 8, 1908.
3. *Ibid.*
4. Author's Correspondence with Buck and Meadows, July 3, 1988.
5. *Ibid.*
6. Pinkerton Files, two letters from Wm. A. Pinkerton to L.L. Lintner in St. Louis, dated April 11, 1919 and November 17, 1921.
7. *Ibid.*
8. *Ibid.*
9. Bolivian Foreign Office Files for 1910, National Archives Records, Washington, D.C.
10. Author's Correspondence with Buck and Meadows.
11. Bolivian Foreign Office Files for 1910, National Archives Records, Washington, D.C.
12. *Ibid.*
13. *Ibid.*
14. *Ibid.*
15. Emma Longabough's Will, copy in author's possession.

Part Four

Appendix

Chapter Twenty-Three

Harry Jr.

He claimed to be the son of the Sundance Kid, but he never produced a birth certificate. He always answered to Harry Jr., but he also gave a number of other names in his various interviews. Among those were Robert Harvey Longabaugh, Harry Thayne Longabaugh, and Harry Longabaugh II. Who was he really?

Shortly after the hit movie was released, Harry Jr. began wandering through the West, giving interviews to local newspapers and lectures at local historical societies and libraries. He told of Sundance's exploits in great detail and of how Sundance had returned to the States from South America.

Harry Jr. claimed to be the grandson of immigrants from Frankfurt, Germany.[1] Sundance's parents and grandparents were all American-born.[2] Depending upon which interview is being researched, Harry Jr. was born five months after Sundance sailed for South America (February 21, 1901).[3] Or his birthdate was February 2, 1901;[4] or he was born January 4, 1901, just before Sundance and Ethel left for South America.[5] He was born in Cimarron, Texas; Cimarron, New Mexico; or Conconcully, Washington.[6] But none of these dates or places were ever proven.

Except for one instance, Harry Jr. claimed his mother was Anna Marie Thayne.[7] In this one exception, Harry Jr. said his mother was *Etta Place*, but he said her real name was either Mary Tryone or Hazel Tryon Johnson Smith.[8] He also said Ethel was a housewife from Castle Gate, Utah, and that she deserted her family to follow Sundance to South America.[9] He said that she left two young children behind. After she supposedly returned to the States in 1906, he said she looked for her children, unsuccessfully.[10] Harry Jr. said Ethel then settled in Marion, Oregon, where she died in 1949.[11] However, researchers cannot find any proof of this information.

Harry Jr. claimed Anna Marie Thayne was a school teacher, and she was the step or half-sister of Ethel Place.[12] He said Anna's parents were Mr. and Mrs. Howard Harold Thayne of Carbon County, Utah.[13] Researcher Pearl Baker said there are many Thayne's in Carbon County, but she never found any Anna Marie or Howard H. Thayne.[14] Harry Jr. also once claimed that his parents met and married in Price, Utah, in 1899.[15] Price is in Carbon County, near Castle Gate, and is in an area which was frequented by Sundance; but no proof has ever been found for this information either.

Harry Jr. also claimed that his parents met and married in San Francisco, California.[16] Sundance did often visit his brother, Elwood, there; and Harry Jr. said his mother was visiting there with a girlfriend.[17] He said the wedding ceremony was on a ship at sea on June 18, 1899.[18] That type of wedding, however, would seem more likely for Elwood, the sailor, than for Sundance, the cowboy. The date also would have been difficult for Sundance since he had just robbed the train in Wilcox, Wyoming, on June 2, 1899.[19]

Whoever his mother was, Harry Jr. claimed that she divorced Sundance in the state of Washington after he went to South America with Ethel.[20] His mother then died in a horse and wagon accident in 1903 in Washington, and Harry Jr. was raised by family friends named Nielon.[21] However, he also claimed on different occasions to have been raised by his mother's family in either Colorado, Texas, New Mexico, Washington, Idaho, or Wyoming.[22]

Harry Jr. told many stories of his father's return to the United States. He claimed Sundance originally returned in 1912 and spent some time in Alaska after winning a placer mine while playing cards.[23] Harry Jr. claimed he first met Sundance in 1940 at the old Chicago Hotel in Spokane, Washington.[24] He had supposedly gone there after a chance meeting with Butch Cassidy in Jackson Hole, Wyoming, and hearing that Sundance was looking for him.[25]

On another occasion, however, Harry Jr. said that he had first met Sundance in Baggs, Wyoming in 1934. He then spent four days with Sundance in Chicago.[26] During their visits, Sundance supposedly told Harry Jr. a number of generally unknown things about the old Wild Bunch. He also supposedly gave Harry Jr. maps to about $300,000 in buried loot.[27] Harry Jr. claimed to have once dug up $6000 in 1940 at Idaho's Bruneau Canyon. He said it was money from a 1900 Nevada bank job. Winnemucca could fit that description and area.[28] Harry Jr. claimed he never searched for the rest of the cached money because treasury agents were always on his trail.[29]

Harry Jr. first said that his father died in 1957; later in the same lecture he said it was 1958.[30] Once he even gave an exact date, August 28, 1957.[31] Sundance was supposedly buried in Casper, Wyoming[32] under either the name Harry Long or Frank Jones.[33] Although Harry Jr. claimed to have eventually found a grave, no researcher has ever been able to verify this.[34]

So far we have seen mostly unproven claims and inaccuracies in Harry Jr.'s interviews. However, when detailing some of Sundance's robberies, Harry Jr. gave some new information from the Winnemucca bank job. He claimed his mother went along and held a horse relay for this job.[35] After the robbery, Butch, Sundance, and Harry Jr.'s mother headed for Bruneau Canyon, Idaho. From there, Sundance and his wife went to Yureka, California, and then on to San Francisco.[36]

When Harry Jr. was being interviewed in Hanksville, Utah, he claimed to know where one of the Robbers Roost cabins was located.[37] He said that his father had told him how to find it. None of the local residents believed Harry Jr. because they knew the old cabins had all fallen in disrepair years before. Harry Jr. insisted, however, and took author Pearl Baker's son, Noel, out to the cabin. Noel could not believe his eyes, saying he had never noticed it in all his years of growing up and living in the area. There were even some old outlaw names scrawled into the wood.[38]

Harry Jr. was also the first person to suggest that Butch Cassidy had lived in Spokane, Washington, under the name of William T. Phillips.[39] A number of articles and a book have since been written about Mr. Phillips.[40]

So, why did Harry Jr. obviously know some things and yet not know other things of equal interest and importance? The family inaccuracies might be because Harry Jr. had almost no time with either of his parents. His mother had either deserted him or had died when he was quite young, and she may not even have known Sundance or his family long herself. The family who raised Harry Jr. probably knew very little, or they may not have wanted to tell him anything. The other discrepancies may have been just a lack of proper research by Harry Jr., whether his claims were sincere or fraudulent. Some researchers believe that he may have been, or closely known, someone on the fringes of the Wild Bunch. He therefore could have picked up some correct details and missed or forgotten other facts.

Harry Jr. died on December 18, 1972, in Missoula, Montana.[41] He died trying to escape a fire in the Priess Hotel, where he was living. The many articles of proof which Harry claimed to be collecting were apparently lost in the fire.[42] There was some suspicion that the fire, which began directly under Harry Jr.'s room, was deliberately set, but an investigation was never completed.[43]

Harry Jr.'s death certificate and the county welfare funeral records provided a surprising amount of information.[44] According to these records, Robert Harvey Longabaugh was born January 4, 1901, in Cimarron, New Mexico. His parents were listed as Harold Longabaugh and Mary Tryone, and he had a relative named John Harold Longabaugh, whose whereabouts were known. He collected welfare under his Social Security number 526-15-2513. Finally, he was buried in the Missoula Cemetery with a Pastor from the Baptist Church presiding.[45]

While none of my research has found any of the Longabaugh's listed above, the name *Harvey* is certainly one of our family names. And although Harry Jr. may not have been a very religious man, welfare records indicate that he must have kept somewhat to our family's Baptist teachings.[46] Lastly, and possibly most convincing to me, Harry Jr.'s photographs bear much too strong a family resemblance for the family to discredit or disown him.

Who was Harry Jr.? Maybe he really was a son of the Sundance Kid. Maybe he was a son of Seth Longabaugh, the cousin listed in the Pinkerton files. Or maybe he was an unknown son of Elwood Longabaugh, Sundance's older brother.

194

Chapter Twenty-Three

But, whoever he was, or whatever his name, he was a Longabaugh.

Notes

1. Jim Dullenty, "The Strange Case of Sundance Kid Junior," *Newsletter of the National Association and Center for Outlaw and Lawman History.*
2. Private Family Records.
3. *The Daily Press* (Craig, Colorado), January 16, 1973.
4. *Sun Advocate* (Price, Utah), July 23, 1970.
5. Dullenty, op cit.
6. *Ibid.*
7. *Sun Advocate* (Price, Utah), July 23, 1970; Harry Longabaugh, Jr., Weber County Library Lecture, (Ogden, Utah), June 24, 1970, transcript supplied by Esther Campbell.
8. *Ibid*; *Sun Advocate* (Price, Utah), July 23, 1970.
9. *Ibid*; Longabaugh, op cit.
10. *Ibid.*
11. *Ibid.*
12. *Sun Advocate* (Price, Utah), July 23, 1970.
13. Dullenty, op cit.
14. Author's interview with Pearl Baker, April 18, 1988.
15. Dullenty, op cit.
16. *Ibid.*
17. *Ibid.*
18. *Ibid.*
19. Pinkerton Files.
20. *Sun Advocate* (Price, Utah), July 23, 1970; *The Daily Press* (Craig, Colorado), January 16, 1973.
21. Dullenty, op cit; Longabaugh, op cit.
22. Dullenty, op cit.
23. *The Daily Press* (Craig, Colorado), January 16, 1973; *Sun Advocate* (Price, Utah), July 23, 1970.
24. *Ibid*; Dullenty, op cit.
25. *Sun Advocate* (Price, Utah), July 23, 1970.
26. *The Daily Press* (Craig, Colorado), January 16, 1973.
27. *The Sunday Missoulian*, October 3, 1971.
28. *United Press International* news release, December 20, 1972; *The Sunday Missoulian*, October 3, 1971.
29. *Ibid.*
30. *United Press International* news release, December 20, 1972; Longabaugh, op cit.
31. *San Jose Mercury*, December 25, 1972; *The Sunday Missoulian*, October 3, 1971.
32. *The Daily Press* (Craig, Colorado), January 16, 1973.
33. Dullenty, op cit.

34. Longabaugh, op cit.
35. Dullenty, op cit.
36. *Ibid.*
37. Author's interview with Pearl Baker, April 18, 1988; author's interview with Barbara Ekker, April 19, 1988.
38. *The Sunday Missoulian*, October 3, 1971; author's interview with Pearl Baker, April 18, 1988.
39. *United Press International* news release, December 20, 1972; *The Sunday Missoulian*, October 3, 1971.
40. Pointer, op cit, pages vii-ix; Dullenty, op cit.
41. Montana State Death Certificate #72-6562, supplied by Norma Hurd.
42. *San Jose Mercury*, December 25, 1972.
43. Dullenty, op cit.
44. Montana State Death Certificate #72-6562; The National Funeral Record #6-108; and *Missoula County Welfare Records*; all supplied by Norma Hurd.
45. *Ibid.*
46. *Ibid.*

Chapter Twenty-Four

Longabaugh Genealogy

First Generation

101 - Conrad Langenbach was born in the 1750's in Germany. He immigrated to America as an indentured servant, arriving in Philadelphia, Pennsylvania 24 December 1772 aboard the Brig *Morning Star*. His contract was bought by John Hunter of Coventry Township, Chester County, Pennsylvania; and it called for Conrad to work for five years as an apprentice or buy his freedom for 28.2 pounds. Conrad later served two months in the militia in Northampton County, Pennsylvania, during the Revolutionary War. In 1781, Conrad married Catharina and settled in NewHanover, Montgomery County, Pennsylvania. Conrad and Catharina had at least the following children:

201 - Catharina Longabaugh
202 - Elizabeth Longabaugh
203 - Maria Magdalena Longabaugh
204 - Henrich Longabaugh
205 - Samuel Longabaugh
206 - Jonas Longabaugh
207 - Lydia Longabaugh

Second Generation

201 - Catharina Longabaugh (of Conrad[1]) was born 8 December 1782 in Montgomery County, Pennsylvania.

202 - Elizabeth Longabaugh (of Conrad[1]) was born ca 1784 in Montgomery County, Pennsylvania. She married 12 October 1800 Joh. Reiher.

203 - Maria Magdalena Longabaugh (of Conrad[1]) was born 7 January 1785 in Montgomery County, Pennsylvania.

204 - Henrich Longabaugh (of Conrad[1]) was born in 1787 in Montgomery County, Pennsylvania; he died 8 April 1795 at age 7.

205 - Samuel Longabaugh (of Conrad[1]) was born 28 September 1796 in Montgomery County, Pennsylvania.

206 - Jonas Longabaugh (of Conrad[1]) was born ca 1797-8 in Montgomery County, Pennsylvania. He married Christiana Hillbert, daughter of Michael and Elizabeth Hillbert, on 6 December 1821 in Pennsylvania. She was born 30 January 1800, and died 12 September 1852, of uterine cancer. Jonas died 28 June 1864 in Upper Providence Township, Pennsylvania. They are both buried in the St. Luke Reformed Church Cemetery, Trappe, Pennsylvania. Jonas owned at least three properties: a property on Railroad Street in Phoenixville, Pennsylvania, was deeded to his daughter Mrs. Margaret Higgins on 1 November 1849; an adjacent property was deeded to another daughter

Mrs. Mary O'Donnell at the same time; property at the intersection of Egypt Road and the current Route #29 in Mont Clare, Pennsylvania, belonged to Jonas according to a town map drawn in 1860. Jonas and Christiana Longabaugh had the following children:

301 - Josiah Longabaugh
302 - Nathaniel H. Longabaugh
303 - Michael Longabaugh
304 - Mary E. Longabaugh
305 - Margaret Longabaugh
306 - "Infant", stillborn Longabaugh

207 - Lydia Longabaugh (of Conrad[1]) was born 25 December 1800 in Montgomery County, Pennsylvania.

Third Generation

301 - Josiah Longabaugh (of Jonas[2] Conrad[1]) was born 14 June 1822 in Pennsylvania. Josiah married Ann G. Place on 11 August 1855 in Phoenixville, Pennsylvania, the Rev. J.S. Ermentrout presiding. Annie was born 27 September 1828, the daughter of Henry and Rachel (Tustin) Place. Annie died of heart disease 18 May 1887; and Josiah died of heart disease 9 August 1893. They are buried in the Morris Cemetery in Phoenixville, Pennsylvania, in a plot owned by the Hallman family. Josiah and Annie Longabaugh had the following children:

401 - Elwood Place Longabaugh
402 - Samanna Longabaugh
403 - Emma T. Longabaugh

404 - Harvey Sylvester Longabaugh

405 - Harry A. Longabaugh

302 - Nathaniel H. Longabaugh (of Jonas[2] Conrad[1]) was born ca 1824-5 in Pennsylvania. He married Asenath Wood about 1857. Asenath died in July 1908; and Nathaniel died in February 1909 in Camden, New Jersey. He had pursued many careers, among which were hotel keeper, school teacher, physician, and farmer. Nathaniel and Asenath had the following children:

406 - Adel Longabaugh

407 - William Wood Longabaugh

303 - Michael Longabaugh (of Jonas[2] Conrad[1]) was born 11 November 1825 in Zeiglersville, Pennsylvania. He married Elizabeth Kane, who was born in 1838 in Pennsylvania. Michael died 18 April 1908 in Upper Providence, Pennsylvania; and Elizabeth died in 1921. They are buried in Morris Cemetery in Phoenixville, Pennsylvania. Michael worked as a farmer, schoolteacher, and boat captain on the Schuylkill Canal. He also ran a feed store at Church and Main Streets,Phoenixville, Pennsylvania.Michael and Elizabeth Longabaugh had the following children:

408 - Emma I. Longabaugh

409 - Sallie A. Longabaugh

304 - Mary E. Longabaugh (of Jonas[2] Conrad[1]) was born 31 January 1831 in Pennsylvania. She first married Patrick O'Donnell; second she married Daniel Weikel. She died 16 February 1857 and is

buried with her parents in St. Luke's Cemetery in Trappe, Pennsylvania.

Daniel and Elizabeth Weikel had the following child:

410 - Mary Ann Elizabeth Weikel

305 - Margaret Longabaugh (of Jonas[2] Conrad[1]) married John Higgins.

Fourth Generation

401 - Elwood Place Longabaugh (of Josiah[3] Jonas[2] Conrad[1]) was born 21 June 1858 in Mont Clare, Pennsylvania. He sailed on the Whaling Ship *Mary & Helen* on 27 June 1882 and landed and settled in San Francisco, California, where he worked at the La Guna Honda Home for Sailors. He died of a coronary and bronchial pneumonia 11 May 1930 at the hospital in the Home. He is buried in Woodlawn Cemetery in San Francisco, California.

402 - Samanna Longabaugh (of Josiah[3] Jonas[2] Conrad[1]) was born 22 April 1860 in Phoenixville, Pennsylvania. She married Oliver F. Hallman in 1878 in Phoenixville. Oliver was born 20 February 1856 in Phoenixville to Augustus and Mary (Conklin) Hallman. Samanna died in 1920 at her home on Walnut Street in Mont Clare, Pennsylvania; and Oliver died 24 November 1941, in Upland, Pennsylvania. Oliver and Samana Hallman had the following children:

501 - A. Adella Hallman
502 - Furman ("Bud") A. Hallman
503 - Bertha Viola Hallman
504 - Granville L. Hallman
505 - Emma Elva Hallman

403 - Emma T. Longabough (of Josiah[3] Jonas[2] Conrad[1]) was born ca 1862-3 in Zeiglersville, Pennsylvania. She died unwed 23 January 1933 in Upper Providence Township Pennsylvania, and is buried with her parents in the Morris Cemetery, Phoenixville, Pennsylvania. She co-owned a dress shop, McCandless and Longabough, on Poplar Street in Philadelphia, Pennsylvania.

404 - Harvey Sylvester Longabough (of Josiah[3] Jonas[2] Conrad[1]) was born 19 May 1865 in Upper Providence Township, Pennsylvania. Harvey married Katherine Gercke in 1886-7. Katherine was born 1 October 1865, and her mother's name was Suzanne. Harvey died 6/7 January 1937 in Wyndmoor, Pennsylvania; Katherine died in 1949 in Ardsley, Pennsylvania. They are buried in Zion Cemetery, Flourtown, Pennsylvania. Harvey worked as a farmer, general-store merchant, iron worker, and carpenter. The family lived in Phoenixville, Flourtown, Providence Township, Haycock Township, Zeiglersville, Skip-pack, and Mont Clare, Pennsylvania, and Atlantic City, New Jersey but never owned a home or stayed in one place for a very long time. Harvey and Katherine Longabough had the following children:

506 - Harvey Sylvester Longabough
507 - William Henry Longabough
508 - Florence A. Longabough

405 - Harry A. Longabaugh (of Josiah[3] Jonas[2] Conrad[1]) was born in the spring of 1867 in Port Providence, Upper Providence Township, Pennsylvania. He became better known by his alias, the Sundance Kid. He may have married Anna Marie Thayne of Utah and had a son *Harry Jr.* around 1901. He married Ethel who went to South America with him in 1901. He died 8 November 1908 in Bolivia

406 - Adel Longabaugh (of Nathaniel[3] Jonas[2] Conrad[1]) was born in 1859 in Pennsylvania. She married J.N. Woolman, a pharmacist; and they lived in Camden, New Jersey.

407 - William Wood Longabaugh (of Nathaniel[3] Jonas[2] Conrad[1]) was born in 1859-60 in Pennsylvania. He married Anna Hurst, and they lived in Reading and Allentown, Pennsylvania. William died in 1931, and Anna died in 1946. They are buried in Montgomery Cemetery, Norristown, Pennsylvania. William and Anna Longabaugh had at least the following child:

509 - Adele H. Longabaugh

408 - Emma Ida Longabaugh (of Michael[3] Jonas[2] Conrad[1]) was born in 1861 in Pennsylvania. She once maintained a millinery shop in Phoenixville, Pennsylvania, and was extremely close with her cousins Samanna and Emma Longabaugh. She died unwed 26 February 1944 in Mont Clare, Pennsylvania, and she is buried with her parents in the Morris Cemetery in Phoenixville, Pennsylvania.

409 -   Sallie A. ("Sarah") Longabaugh (of Michael³ Jonas²
         Conrad¹) was born in 1864 in Pennsylvania. She
         married __?__ Hemsher and divorced him soon
         thereafter. She was so close to her cousins
         Samanna and Emma that she was often thought
         to be a sister. She died in 1947 and is buried with
         her parents in Morris Cemetery, Phoenixville,
         Pennsylvania.

410 -   Mary Ann Elizabeth Weikel (of Mary³ Jonas²
         Conrad¹) died as an infant 31 July 1857 and is
         buried with her mother in the St. Luke's Cem-
         etery in Trappe, Pennsylvania.

Fifth Generation

501 -   A. Adella Hallman (of Samanna⁴ Josiah³ Jonas²
         Conrad¹) was born 18 October 1879 in Mont
         Clare, Pennsylvania. She married Henry L.
         Webber. She died on 24 September 1902 and was
         buried in Morris Cemetery in Phoenixville, Penn-
         sylvania.

502 -   Furman ("Bud") A. Hallman (of Samanna⁴ Josiah³
         Jonas² Conrad¹) was born 25 October 1880 in
         Mont Clare, Pennsylvania. He married Adelaide
         T. Sturgis, and they had at least one child, Wil-
         liam Hallman. Furman died 9 June 1969.

503 -   Bertha Viola Hallman (of Samanna⁴ Josiah³
         Jonas² Conrad¹) was born 13 December 1881 in
         Mont Clare, Pennsylvania. She died 5 January
         1882.

504 -   Granville L. Hallman (of Samanna⁴ Josiah³ Jonas²
         Conrad¹) was born 2 April 1885 in Mont Clare,

*William Henry Longabough (left) our grandfather
and the nephew of Sundance; Harvey S.
Longabough, Jr. (right) taken in 1914. (Courtesy
William D. Longabough.)*

Pennsylvania. He married Alice Brower, and they had children. Granville died 18 August 1963.

505 - Emma Elva Hallman (of Samanna[4] Josiah[3] Jonas[2] Conrad[1]) was born 29 July 1887, and died 26 January 1888.

506 - Harvey Sylvester Longabough (of Harvey[4] Josiah[3] Jonas[2] Conrad[1]) was born in 1888. He died unwed in 1915 and was buried in Zion Cemetery in Flourtown, Pennsylvania, with his parents and sister.

507 - William Henry Longabough (of Harvey[4] Josiah[3] Jonas[2] Conrad[1]) was born 28 October 1893 in Philadelphia, Pennsylvania. He married Rose Sophie Sippel on 9 April 1917 in Philadelphia. Rose had been born 3 June 1897 in Philadelphia to Carolyn "Lena" Sippel, an immigrant from

William Henry Longabough, son of Harvey S. Longabaugh, nephew of Sundance with his wife Rose, and baby daughter Florence circa 1925. (Courtesy Paul D. Ernst.)

Germany. They lived in Ardsley, Pennsylvania, where Bill worked as a mechanic and carpenter. Bill died of heart disease on 9 March 1976 in Abington, Pennsylvania; and Rose died of heart disease on 1 July 1977 in Cheltenham, Pennsylvania. They are both buried at Hillside Cemetery in Roslyn, Pennsylvania. Bill and Rose Longabough had the following children:

601 - William Henry Longabough
602 - Florence Catherine Longabough
603 - William David Longabough

508 - Florence A. Longabough (of Harvey[4] Josiah[3] Jonas[2] Conrad[1]) was born in 1896 in Pennsylvania. She died of a ruptured appendix in 1910 and was buried with her parents and brother in Zion Cemetery, Flourtown, Pennsylvania.

*Bill and Rose Longabough circa 1946 with
their grandchildren Jean and Paul Ernst.
(Courtesy Paul D. Ernst.)*

207

509 - Adele H. Longabaugh (of William[4] Nathaniel[3] Jonas[2] Conrad[1]) was born 1886 in Pennsylvania, died in 1891. She is buried with her parents in Montgomery Cemetery, Norristown, Pennsylvania.

Sixth Generation

601 - William Henry Longabough (of William[5] Harvey[4] Josiah[3] Jonas[2] Conrad[1]) was born in April 1918 in Ardsley, Pennsylvania. He died within a week and is buried in Zion Cemetery, Flourtown, Pennsylvania.

602 - Florence Catherine Longabough (of William5 Harvey[4] Josiah[3] Jonas[2] Conrad[1]) was born 31 May 1919 in Ardsley, Pennsylvania. She married Harry Herman Ernst of Philadelphia, Pennsylvania, 31 August 1940. Harry was born 19 June 1918 in Philadelphia to Harry S. and Marie Frances (Aschendorf) Ernst. Florence died of heart failure 27 August 1980 in Ardsley, Pennsylvania and is buried in Hillside Cemetery, Roslyn, Pennsylvania. Harry and Florence Ernst had the following children, all born in Pennsylvania:

701 - Jean Elaine Ernst; born 1 March 1942
702 - Paul David Ernst; born 3 June 1945
703 - Harry Herman Ernst; born 19 August 1953

603 - William David Longabough (of William[5] Harvey[4] Josiah[3] Jonas[2] Conrad[1]) was born 29 August 1929 in Ardsley, Pennsylvania. He married Dorothy Wilson 9 May 1953, and legally adopted Karin, Dorothy's daughter from her first marriage.

Sundance, Etta and Dog in Cholila, Argentina.
(Copyright Paul D. Ernst.)

The Longabaugh family name has died out in Sundance's
direct lineage.

Bibliography

Baker, Pearl; *The Wild Bunch at Robbers Roost*, Abelard-Schuman, 1971.

Bankston, Wilma Crisp; *Where Eagles Winter*.

Basso, Dave; *Ghosts of Humboldt Region*, Western Printing & Publishing Co., 1970.

Bean, editor; *Montgomery County History*.

Berk, Lee; "Who Robbed the Winnemucca Bank?," *Quarterly of the National Association and Center for Outlaw and Lawman History*, 1983.

Betenson, Lula Parker; *Butch Cassidy, My Brother*, Brigham Young University Press, 1984.

Brand Book of the Montana Stock Growers Association, Montana Stock Growers Association.

Brekke, Alan Lee; *Kid Curry: Train Robber*, Harlem News/Chinook Opinion, 1989.

Briehan, Carl W.; *Wild Women of the West*, Signet Brand Western, 1982.

Brown and Felton; *Before Barbed Wire*, Bramhall House, 1956.

Buck, Dan and Anne Meadows; "Wild Bunch Rampage in South America," *Quarterly of the National Association and Center for Outlaw and Lawman History*, Vol. XII, Nos. 3 and 4.

Button, I. Victor; "Butch Cassidy Gave Getaway Horse to 10-Year-Old," *Newsletter of the National Association and Center for Outlaw and Lawman History*.

Campbell, Charles F.; unpublished collection of Livestock History, Montana Historical Society.

Chapman, Arthur; "Butch Cassidy," *The Elks Magazine*, April, 1930.

Chatwin, Bruce; *In Patagonia*, Penguin Books, 1977.

Churchill, E. Richard; *They Rode with Butch Cassidy, The McCartys*, B & B Printers, 1972.

Cornelison, John; "The Wilcox Train Robbery" unpublished collection, Wyoming State Archives, Historical Research Department.

Cude, Elton R.; *The Blue Book*, 1911.

Curtis, Albert; *Fabulous San Antonio*, The Naylor Co., 1955.

Drucker, Edward A.; "Witness Recalls Chasing Robbers," *The Humboldt Sun*, September 16, 1982

Dullenty, Jim; "The Strange Case of Sundance Kid Junior," *Newsletter of the National Association and Center for Outlaw and Lawman History*.

Ellis, Fern D.; *Come Back to My Valley*.

Family Records; family-owned Bibles, journals, letters, and interviews have been used to verify some previously unknown stories and events. These items and the family photos are being used on a one-time basis only for this book.

Engebretson, Doug; *Empty Saddles, Forgotten Names*, North Plains Press, 1984.

Freeman, Ira S.; *A History of Montezuma County*, Johnson Publishing Co., 1958.

French, Captain William, *Recollections of a Western Ranchman*, High-Lonesome Books, reprint 1990.

From Buffalo Bones to Sonic Boom, Glasgow Jubilee Committee, 1962.

Garman, Mary; "Harry Longabaugh — The Sundance Kid, The Early Years, 1867-1889," *Bits and Pieces*, 1977.

German Indentured Servants, Genealogical Publication.

Head, June, editor; *Our One Hundred Years of Banking in Montezuma County*, Beaber Printing Company, 1986.

Henry, Ralph C.; *Our Land Montana*, State Publishing Co., 1969.

Horan, James D.; *The Outlaws*, Crown Publishing Inc., 1977.

Horan, James D. and Paul Sann; *Pictorial History of the Wild West*, Crown Publishing Inc., 1954.

Irish, Donna R.; *Pennsylvania German Marriages*, Genealogical Publishing Co., Inc., 1982.

Jessen, Kenneth; *Colorado Gunsmoke*.

Kelly, Charles; *The Outlaw Trail, The Story of Butch Cassidy and The Wild Bunch*, Bonanza Books, 1959.

Kirby, Edward M.; *The Rise & Fall of the Sundance Kid*, Western Publishers, 1983.

Kelsey, Michael R.; *Henry Mountains and Robbers Roost*, Kelsey Publishing, 1987.

Kline, Rev. J.J.; *History of the Lutheran Church*, New Hanover, Pennsylvania, 1910.

Kouris, Diana Allen; *The Romantic and Notorious History of Brown's Park*, The Wolverine Gallery, 1988.

Lamb, F. Bruce, *Kid Curry, The Life and Times of Harvey Logan and the Wild Bunch*, Johnson Books, 1991.

Longabaugh, Harry Jr.; Weber County Library, Lecture transcript, June 24, 1970.

McCarty, Tom; *Tom McCarty's Own Story, Autobiography of an Outlaw*, Rocky Mt. House, 1986.

McLoughlin, Denis; *The Wild and Woolly, An Encyclopedia of the Old West*, Doubleday and Company, 1975.

Menefee, George W.; *Cow Talk*, memoirs as recorded by Lottie W. Reddert.

Mokler, Alfred James, *The History of Natrona County, Wyoming 1888-1922*, R.R. Donnelley & Sons Company, 1923.

Morgan, Dale L.; *The Humboldt, Highroad of the West*, J.J. Little and Ives Co., 1943.

Neidringhaus, A.W.; unpublished collection of Livestock History, Montana Historical Society.

Paher, Stanley W.; *Nevada Ghost Towns & Mining Camps*, Howell-North Books, 1970.

Paher, Stanley W.; *Nevada Towns & Tales, Vol. I*-North, Nevada Publications, 1981.

Patterson, Richard; *Historical Atlas of the Outlaw West*, Johnson Books, 1985.

Pennsylvania Archives, *Associators and Militia*, Genealogical Publication.

Pennsylvania German Pioneers, Genealogical Publication.

Perkins, Nielson, & Jones; *Saga of San Juan Valley*, San Juan County Daughters of Utah Pioneers, 1957.

Piernes, Justin; "Butch Cassidy en la Patagonia," *Clarin*, May 2, 3 and 4, 1970.

Pointer, Larry; *In Search of Butch Cassidy*, University of Oklahoma, 1977.

Rupp, Prof. I. Daniel; *Immigrants in Pennsylvania*.

Sanders, Leonard; *How Fort Worth Became The Texasmost City*, Amon Carter Museum of Western Art, 1973.

Segars, Loretta; *100 Years in Culbertson*, Culbertson Centennial Steering Committee, 1986.

Selcer, Richard F.; *Hell's Half Acre*, TCU Press, 1991.

Siringo, Charles A.; *A Cowboy Detective*, University of Nebraska Press, 1988.

Swallow, Alan, editor; *The Wild Bunch*, Sage Books, 1966.

Tennent, William L.; *John Jarvie of Brown's Park*, Utah Bureau of Land Management, 1982.

Thompson and West; *History of Nevada 1881,* Howell-North, 1958.

Toll, David W.; "Butch Cassidy & The Great Winnemucca Bank Robbery," *Nevada*, May/June 1983.

Van Dersal & Connor; *Stockgrowers Directory of Marks and Brands*, Van Dersal & Connor.

Warner, Matt; *The Last of the Bandit Riders*, Bonanza Books, 1950.

Index

Index

Index

About the Author . . .

When Donna Ernst spoke at the Denver meeting of the Western Outlaw-Lawman History Association in the summer of 1992 she told how she discovered that the Sundance Kid was her husband Paul's great-uncle. Donna and Paul spent a summer vacation roaming through the western United States without realizing that there were Pennsylvania Longaboughs who had come before them.

When Paul and I got married twenty-five years ago, our first real vacation was a trip out West. We visited Mesa Verde (near Robbers Roost), the Badlands and Custer's Last Stand (near Sundance, Wyoming), and even the Rock Candy Mountain. (near Circleville, Utah). But we never knew how close to our own history we were. We were only looking at the scenery and historic sights.

We had no idea who Harry Longabaugh was. We had never heard of either the Sundance Kid or Butch Cassidy. We just had a love of history, we enjoyed traveling, and we had a fascination for the west.

By this time I was already very much into genealogy . . . Mom's father, William Longabough, kept telling me there weren't any other relatives alive . . . So as far as I knew, there was absolutely no family or history.

By 1976, Grandpop was in failing health. During one visit with his son (our Uncle Bill) Grandpop asked him why he had no interest in the family history. Uncle Bill replied that he did, but that Grandpop never told anyone anything.

Grandpop then said, "Well, I had two uncles who were like Jesse James and died in South America . . . " After Uncle Bill had caught his breath enough to ask for details, Grandpop said "it really wasn't anyone's business and forget about it." So Uncle Bill dropped the subject. But Grandpop went senile in his last few months, and he repeated the story to Uncle Bill more than once. Regretfully, Uncle Bill thought he was out of his head and never mentioned the stories to me.

Well, Grandpop soon died, in March of 1976, never having told anyone what all he knew. He died in silence, taking his

Sundance, My Uncle

The author in San Antonio, Texas. (Courtesy Sundance Prop.)

memories with him. Then in November of that year, Robert Redford had an article about the Outlaw Trail in The National Geographic. Uncle Bill was at a church supper when a friend came up to him...and she called him Sundance.

Uncle Bill couldn't imagine what she was talking about, so she explained about seeing the article . . . The next week, Uncle Bill borrowed a copy of the magazine and contacted Paul and me.

This article started a search for the trails ridden earlier by Sundance. On research trips out west, each spot discovered held special meaning. Hours were spent in the Pinkerton files, in public libraries, going anywhere that claimed " . . . Sundance slept here."

So, while I am certainly not a professional writer . . . I think you can see that I love history and I don't mind doing a lot of research. I have mixed my desire to accuracy and my access to private family information together with the historical details of Sundance's life. In the process I have found some new information . . . and I have corrected a few inaccuracies.

Donna and Paul Ernst live in Sellersville, Pennsylvania, only about ten miles from her husband's Longabaugh relatives in Phoenixville. Donna and Paul have three daughters, Jennifer, Susan, and Janice.

Books Available From The Early West

The Earps Talk by Alford Turner. The Earp brothers, Wyatt, Virgil and James tell the story in their own words. Annotated primary source material from newspapers, court records and official documents. 195 pp., index, illus., maps. Hardcover **$19.95**

The O.K. Corral Inquest edited by Alford Turner. For the first time, the complete testimonies of the participants and witnesses heard at the Coroner's Inquest and the month-long Wells Spicer Hearing that followed. Based on a rare transcription made in 1930 of the original court records which have since disappeared. 195 pp., illus., biblio. Hardcover. **$19.95**

The Earp Decision by Jack DeMattos. Wyatt Earp's decision in the heavyweight championship bout between Robert Fitzsimmons and Tom Sharkey on December 2, 1896 catapulted him into the national headlines and led him into court and days of controversy in the newspapers. 205 pp., index, biblio., notes, contemporary cartoon illus. Hardcover. **$21.95**

Mysterious Gunfighter: Dave Mather by Jack DeMattos. A gunfighter who was far better known during his lifetime, Mather turns up in Dodge City, Kansas, and Las Vegas, New Mexico when they were the wildest of the wild west. A well-researched, well-written biography of one of the west's most interesting and elusive characters. 185 pp., index, photos, biblio., illus. Hardcover. **$21.95**

Bowen and Hardin by Chuck and Marjorie Parsons. Another look at Texas in the 1870's. Brown Bowen was the badman brother-in-law of John Wesley Hardin, the deadliest gunfighter of all time. Hardin broke Bowen out of jail and Bowen carelessly led the law back to Hardin. 159 pp., index, photos, illus., biblio. Hardcover. **$21.95**

The Capture of Billy the Kid edited by James H. Earle. Two firsthand, unedited accounts of the capture of the Kid at Stinking Springs, New Mexico Territory in December 1880. Also with previously published versions from other participants. 159 pp., index, biblio., photos., illus. Hardcover. **$21.95**

I Buried Billy by A. P. "Paco" Anaya. A firsthand account of Billy the Kid's last days in Fort Sumner, New Mexico. Anaya dictated his memories and his conversations with Billy to his son, Louis Anaya, in 1931. The Anaya family has allowed us to publish this story. 160 pp., index, biblio., photos, illus., the Charlie Foor Map. Hardcover. **$21.95**

Sundance, My Uncle by Donna B. Ernst. The search for the Sundance Kid by a member of his family. The author had access to a family "diary" and some never-before published photographs of the Sundance Kid, Butch Cassidy and Etta Place. 224 pp., more than sixty photos and maps. Hardcover. **$21.95**

1-800-245-5841

THE EARLY WEST

Box 9292, Ph. 409-775-6047
College Station, Texas 77842

More Books from the Early West

The Custer Autograph Album by John M. Carroll and Bob Aldrich. John M. Carroll, collected autographs, photographs, and illustrations of George Armstrong Custer and the men who either served or were associated with him during the Civil War or the Indian Wars, ending with the Battle of the Little Big Horn. Distinctive illustrations are matched with the autograph, brief biography, and analysis of the handwriting of over 100 people who played an important role in Custer's life. 175+ pages. **$24.95**

Bounty Hunter by Rick Miller. In 1877 Jack Duncan, while a Texas Ranger, aided in the capture of John Wesley Hardin, Texas' most deadly and notorious gunfighters. It was through Duncan's ability as a detective that the wily Hardin was found. Jack Duncan spent most of his adult life in Dallas, working as a detective and bounty hunter. He met many of the infamous personalities of his day: Doc Holliday, Frank James, Belle Starr, the Younger brothers, Longhair Jim Courtright and Luke Short. 225 pp., index, biblio., notes, contemporary photos. Hardcover. **$21.95**

Hands Up! The History of a Crime by Al Sorenson. The reprint of an extremely rare book about Sam Bass' first train robbery in Big Spring, Nebraska. 147 pp., with an added index and comments by Wayne Gard, noted Sam Bass biographer, and the original illustrations. Leatherbound, hardcover. **$19.95**

Thrilling Events. Life of Henry Starr by Himself. The reprint of an extremely rare autobiography written in 1914 by one of the boldest of the early bank robbers. As such, Starr lost his life in a daring attempt to rob a bank in Harrison, Arkansas. 95 pp., index, photos. Leatherbound, hardcover. **$19.95**

Jessie Evans: Lincoln County Badman by Grady McCright and James Powell. Evans has been named as the killer of John Tunstall, Billy the Kid's friend and boss. This enemy of the Kid was smart enough to leave Lincoln County sooner than Billy. If the Kid had done so, he might have survived longer than 21 years! 240 pp., index, biblio., maps, photos, illus. Hardcover. **$18.95**

El Paso Lawman: G. W. Campbell by Fred R. Egloff. More than 100 years have passed since the famous shootout in El Paso took place and George Campbell was gunned down. Campbell was the "bad guy" for many years in many books. Fred Egloff has set the record straight. A look at old El Paso in 1881. 141 pp., index, 38 illus., biblio., notes. Hardcover. **$16.95**

Masterson & Roosevelt by Jack DeMattos. William Barclay "Bat" Masterson began his career as a buffalo hunter, Indian fighter, lawman, gunfighter, and adventurer. He was elected sheriff of Ford County, Kansas at the age of 24. You can read about this part of Bat's life in Bob DeArment's excellent biography. DeMattos covers that unique time when Bat served as U.S. Marshal, appointed by that bully president, Theodore Roosevelt. 151 pp., index, illus., biblio. Hardcover. **$18.95**

Garrett & Roosevelt by Jack DeMattos. One of Pat Garrett's admirers was President Theodore Roosevelt. Roosevelt appointed Garrett as collector of customs. This book is based on the correspondence between Garrett and Roosevelt and Mrs. Garrett and Roosevelt after Pat's assassination. 180 pp., index, notes, sources, photos, and illus. Hardcover. **$18.95**